I WANTED T

BORGHILD DAHL

With a Foreword by William L. Benedict Heed of Department of Ophthalmology, Mayo Clime

Published by Snowball Publishing

www.snowballpublishing.com

info@snowballpublishing.com

To UNCLE ENOCH and AUNT ELIZABETH

Contents

Introduction

Dear Reader,

In the timeless exploration of human potential, there are stories that not only inspire but also redefine the boundaries of possibility. Borghild Dahl's journey, chronicled in her remarkable work "I Wanted to See," is one such narrative—a testament to courage, resilience, and the transformative power of perspective.

In my book, "How to Stop Worrying and Start Living," I invite you to discover the incredible story of Borghild Dahl—a story of courage, resilience, and the remarkable power of perspective.

Borghild Dahl's journey is one that defies the limitations imposed by adversity. Despite being practically blind for fifty years, she approached life with a determination that knew no bounds. From her early years, where she memorized the ground to play with other children, to her academic achievements and eventual career as a professor, Dahl's story is a testament to the triumph of the human spirit.

It was at the age of fifty-two, after a groundbreaking operation at the Mayo Clinic, that Dahl's world was transformed. Suddenly, the world around her was infused with newfound clarity and beauty. Even the simplest tasks, like washing dishes, became moments of profound joy and wonder.

As you delve into the pages of "I Wanted to See," prepare to be inspired and uplifted. Through Dahl's eyes, you will discover a world where every moment is a gift, and every challenge is an opportunity for growth. It is a world where the ordinary becomes extraordinary, and where even the smallest joys can fill your heart with gratitude.

Dahl's life was a testament to perseverance in the face of adversity. Afflicted with near-blindness for half a century, she navigated a world shrouded in darkness with unwavering determination.

With each turn of the page, may you find inspiration, and above all, a profound appreciation for the boundless potential that resides within us all.

Sincerely,

Dale Carnegie

Foreword

Desire to succeed is a state of mind molded by events in a person's youth. His reaction to consciousness of impressions within his environment during the growing years directs the course of all his future activities. Physical handicaps materially retard him on the long road toward achievement of the goal of his activities, but it sometimes seems that difficulties are really a challenge to one who seems least endowed with power to succeed. The will to do finds a way. The achievement of a goal over any road is a matter for congratulation. The road to success is strewn with the lost efforts of those who have tried and failed, because their desire to win was weak and their will to achieve withered away. The consultation room is a harbor into which comes a constant succession of middle-aged and older wrecks of human endeavor and passion unable to weather the sea of trouble on which they embarked with hope and perhaps persuasion. For youth is driven, seldom inspired, to meet certain demands, the minimum for comfortable and respectable living.

We in this country have developed to a high degree a mutual respect for the multiform elements in our social state. Whatever one's aim in life may be, so long as it is not detrimental to the general welfare, one is encouraged and helped. We like to see people succeed and we help them to succeed. That, after all, is what we live for.

Particularly is that the life of a physician. Social workers, ministers, teachers, nurses, doctors and many other people devote a lifetime to teaching and training the youth of the nation, who in turn must become the builders of a great social state. In this service the heart of an individual is touched by the personal charm of one who cares. The people of the world are individuals, not just masses of humanity. Every contact between teacher and pupil, doctor and patient, which conveys one spark of helpful influence is the result of an emotional impulse that is infinitely selective and definitely directed, intentional and reciprocal. Mass education in public schools is no exception. Large medical clinics with multiple consultation rooms are adaptations to meet the demands of the times. To both the schools and the clinics go the millions of people, each with an obligation to that society which relentlessly goes on, helpful to the handicapped who are not deterred.

Borghild Dahl came to the Mayo Clinic, and she soon became a personal friend of all who were to meet her and to know her. She had, despite a severe loss of eyesight, succeeded as a student and as a teacher of languages and literature and had helped to educate her sisters and a brother. Ambition to succeed was inborn, driven by a will through years of schooling before the days of sight-saving classes and the many provisions now available in our public schools for the disabled child. Under school conditions that nowadays are considered intolerable, she maintained a better than average scholastic record, and during all her school years she could read a book with large print only by holding it close to her face. She has told in this book why she persisted in the face of discouraging odds, working harder than any of her classmates. She had an objective that was impersonal. That fact is inherent, she does not dwell upon it. She wanted to see. How much more she could have done with the same drive and application and good eyesight! Only in her later years, has she been able to see the bricks in walls and the leaves on trees. She knows what it is, finally, to have clear vision after years of groping in a dim fog. But that isn't the reason for this book. Miss Dahl clearly tells her readers how success was won despite blindness. She tells teachers, doctors, and social workers how to succeed in their work with handicapped children. She teaches teachers. That was her ambition. This book is her achievement.

William L. Benedict
Head of Department of Ophthalmology, Mayo Clinic Rochester, Minnesota

Chapter 1

Summer school was over at the college where I was teaching, and I went to Rochester for a checkup on my eyes. I had been going to the Mayo Clinic for the past twenty years and the two doctors who had been taking care of my eyes were both good friends of mine. They usually liked to chat with me and ask me how I was getting along with my work.

This time I knew at once that something had gone wrong. As soon as Dr. Benedict looked at my eyes, he became silent. Then he took my arm and said we would go into Dr. Pran-gen's office.

They left me alone for a few minutes and I sat wondering what had happened. I knew, of course, that I had very poor eyesight. I had only one eye, and it was so covered with dense scars that I had to do all my seeing through one small opening in the left of the eye. I could see a book, for example, only by holding it up close to my face and by straining my one eye as hard as I could toward the left. However, I had never let my eyes keep me from most of the things I wanted to do. I had led a rather useful and an extremely full and happy life, and this in spite of the fact that—as I had once heard Dr. Benedict tell the great eye specialist Dr. Fuchs of Vienna—I had only 4/60 vision in my eye. People with 6/60 are considered blind.

In the back of my mind there had always lurked a fear of total blindness. In order to overcome this, I had adopted a cheerful, almost hilarious, attitude toward life. In the tussle which my eyes and I had been having with each other, I really believed I had gotten the better of them at last and that they were hardly an inconvenience to me.

But as I sat in Dr. Prangen's office I thought of all the accidents 1 had been having lately in my home town of Sioux Falls: tripping over bumps and stones in the road which I took as a short cut on my way to school when I was late for my classes, speaking to the wrong people in the crowds downtown on Phillips Avenue, and breaking so many of my best dishes at home that in disgust I bought a heavy set of blue and white ones for everyday use.

Dr. Benedict and Dr. Prangen returned to me; and when Dr. Benedict began to speak, his manner was very grave, and his voice sounded strained and unnatural.

"There is a cataract in your eye," he explained to me, "which will have to be removed. Such an operation will be accompanied by great risks. When I begin operating on your eye, there is no telling what I may find there or what will come out of the eye while the cataract is being removed."

Dr. Prangen and a younger man whom I did not know stood by my chair. I could hear them breathe. A buzzer sounded, but no one paid any attention to it.

"Go back to your home in Sioux Falls," Dr. Benedict went on, "and put your affairs in order there. When you find that your vision is entirely gone, come back to us and we'll see what we can do for you."

There was a dead silence.

"No matter what happens, Borghild," Dr. Benedict said after a little, "I am confident that you will be brave enough to carry on. . ."

"Is everything all right?" Mrs. Seem asked as I joined them in the lobby.

The Seems had come up from Harmony with my sister Dorothy, and we were going to have a picnic together in Mayo Park.

"Yes," I said hurriedly. "But let's eat. I'm starving."

"Maybe you won't have to come back to the clinic for a long time," Dorothy said optimistically, "now that your eyes are getting along so well."

I didn't try to answer her.

We drove directly to the park. Dorothy found a shaded table and hurried over to claim it. The sun was beating down and the day was hot.

"You look tired," Anna Seem said. "Why don't you lie down on the bench here and rest for a few minutes while we get things ready? Cover your face with my hat. There— that's better. I know exactly how you feel after having your eyes tested. It gives me a headache for the rest of the day."

But I was not able to lie still on the bench. As soon as Anna went back to the car, I got up and walked off by myself.

Blind. Blind. Blind.

I closed my eye to see how the world was going to look with my sight all gone. But after I opened it again, I knew I wasn't seeing much more than when it was closed.

Since I was in the park, it was easy to guess that all the green around me was grass and trees and shrubs. But it wasn't at all clear which was which. Nor could I decide whether the bright colors in the distance were flowers or the gay summer clothes of visitors at the park. A huge light splotch of something on my right must be the Mayo Auditorium and the smaller splotches, houses surrounding the park. The light ribbons across the green were probably paths or driveways and the shining things farther off, cars. The entire landscape was blurred, and all at once I realized the full meaning of what Dr. Benedict had told me. I was actually seeing almost nothing.

All my life I had tried to take without too much grumbling what Fate had meted out to me and to put aside a longing to possess a pair of clear, sharp eyes that could see as well as those of other people. I had told myself that other people had other troubles. Mine were my eyes.

But not to be able to see at all!

As far back as I could remember, I knew I was different from other children and that this difference was caused by my eyes. This I did not regard particularly as a misfortune, but rather as something in life that was there and had to be accepted just as my little friend Thelma had to make the most of her inability to remember anything long enough to learn the games, we children in the neighborhood played to-

I believe I was born with a naturally happy disposition. My mother said I was a good baby. My life was so crowded with interesting adventures that I couldn't sleep for fear of missing some of it. My mother often told me that she used to worry about me, for she could not understand when I slept. Whenever she made the rounds of our bedrooms during the night to see that we children were all right, I was always awake.

"Why aren't you asleep?" she would ask me.

"I just couldn't."

"But why?"

"I was having so much fun."

"Fun? Doing what?" she would ask curiously.

"Oh, just playing things."

I lived in a world of make-believe after I had been put to bed. Everything that I had learned during the day—things people had said to me or to others, so I overheard them, or things people read to me, or whatever I had been able to observe by myself—came back to me at night. I put it all through the mill of my imagination and ground out for myself wonderful adventures. I was always the principal in these adventures. Sometimes my bed was a boat that took me over the sea to any part of the world that I wanted to be in. Sometimes my bed was a castle in which a fairy princess lived, and I was the fairy princess. Sometimes it was a great hall where I was the performer, holding large audiences spellbound with my music and fine speeches. Sometimes my bed was a gigantic book out of which I was reading stories all of my own invention. And sometimes I was in heaven, where I, in the company of other angels, was visiting with God.

The older I grew, the more involved the dreams became; but there was more plausibility in them, too, after I learned to understand the ways of the grown-ups and what they were saying.

One day my mother dressed me in my best clothes. I was elated at the prospect of an outing.

"We are going to see a very nice man by the name of Dr. Bendeke," my mother told me while we were on the streetcar.

I had never heard of Dr. Bendeke, but there were many things in the world of grown-ups about which I knew nothing. The ride on the streetcar occupied my whole attention.

We came to a large building and were greeted by a gray and rather stem-looking man. He acted as though he knew my mother, and my mother seemed to be acquainted with him; and the strange part of it was that he seemed to know who I was, too.

"She has fared much better than I had hoped," I heard him tell my mother. "She secs enough to get along pretty well after the operation, does she not?"

"Oh yes, we get along very nicely," my mother assured him.

Dr. Bendeke gave me a little package whose wrappings I began at once to open. While I was busy doing this, he and my mother talked together but so low that I couldn't hear what was being said. After considerable difficulty I succeeded in opening the package. Inside I found a flat, round lozenge about the size of a fifty-cent piece.

Dr. Bendeke looked into my eye with a queer kind of class, and he said something about bathing the eye in hot water whenever it was tired and about preserving the sight that was left in it.

On our way home my mother explained to me that Dr. Bendeke was my eye doctor. I was very proud to have an eye doctor, since I had never known anyone who had owned one.

After that my mother often took me to visit Dr. Bendeke. I was always too shy to let him know how proud I was to own him, for he remained very silent and stern in spite of the fact that he continued to give me sweet lozenges every time I went to see him.

It must have been several years after my first visit to Dr. Bendeke that my mother told me one day we were going to visit my eye doctor once more. This time it took much longer than usual on the streetcar; and when we got off, my mother said we were in St. Paul. We were going to see Dr. Boeckmann, she told me. He would be my eye doctor now.

I could not understand how my mother was able to find so many eye doctors for me, especially since I was the only person who owned any at all.

Dr. Boeckmann was a much larger and jollier man than Dr. Bendeke had been. Dr. Boeckmann, too, looked into my eye with a queer kind of glass.

"My God, what a close call! " I heard him exclaim.

He brought me over to a large machine and I sat and looked into it from one side, and he peeked at me from the other. I had to laugh, for I had not played such a queer kind of game before. When we had finished it, Dr. Boeckmann patted my head and kissed me.

After my visit to this new eye doctor my mother bought me a pair of glasses. They were very heavy and had beautiful, shining gold rims. I was delighted. Wearing eyeglasses was even more exciting than having two eye doctors. None of the children I played with wore eyeglasses.

My mother counted herself in a kind of partnership with me while I was learning to adjust myself to the strange world into which I had been born, although she herself had beautiful dark eyes and perfect vision. So, it was as though this handicap of mine was not peculiar to me alone. When my mother was trying to teach me to dress myself—to fit the innumerable buttons into the innumerable buttonholes, which always seemed too small, in my undershirt, under waist, panties, petticoats, dresses, and shoes—she always spoke as though we were both doing it. After I had finished, she taught me to run my fingers up and down the buttons to make sure that they were all in place.

It was hardest to learn how to button my shoes. The round, black, shiny buttons fastened to the leather by two tiny metal rings wobbled so that they were forever slipping away from me when I tried to pull them through the buttonholes on the flaps of my shoes.

Once, while 1 was sitting on the floor bent over so my nose touched my shoes, the steel buttonhook got caught in the lower lid of my good eye. With the handle dangling down on my cheek, I ran to my mother.

"Don't touch it," my mother said quietly, "I'll have it out in a minute."

She set me on a chair and kneeling in front of me, she held my head with one hand and pulled the hook out with the other. After that she brought a pan of hot water from the kitchen and, while I sat on a low stool beside her chair, she bathed my eye with a soft cloth.

"Your eye doesn't hurt now, does it?" she asked me after a little as she dried my face with a towel.

"No," I told her.

"Thank God," she said.

Then she set me on her lap and explained that I must always be sure to grasp the buttonhook firmly by the triangular handle because there was printing there that made it rough and it wouldn't slip easily from my hand. She showed me exactly how I should put the other end, which was smooth and sharp like a crochet hook, tightly around the button on my shoe and draw it right under the buttonhole before I tried to pull the button through the hole with the buttonhook. She had me do this over and over until at last the round, black, shiny buttons, despite their wobbling, no longer eluded my buttonhook and I was able to pull them easily through the buttonholes on the flaps of my shoes.

In learning to clasp a safety pin I held my hand under my mother's, and we did the new trick together, and I could feel rather than see how it was done. By this same tactual method, I learned to open the lock of my purse, the faucet at the sink, the loop on the front gate, and the door of the oven and the ice chest. My mother also taught me to find the keyhole in the front door with my left hand

and to insert the key into the lock with my right one. We went over all the doorknobs both in our home in Minneapolis and in the one at the lake, just to make sure that we knew where they were and how to turn them. Together we fitted the drawers of my dresser into the spaces where they belonged, being careful to find the grooves first; and at the lake we attached the oarlocks to the oars before we tried to fasten them in the boat. All these everyone else might have taken for granted that I could have learned just as any other child did, but my mother knew better, and she taught me so quietly that no one, not even I at the time, realized what she was doing for me.

As I grew older, she spent less time helping me with each particular problem and rather encouraged me to figure things out for myself and to do them alone if it were possible for me.

"Learn to depend upon yourself," she said to me so often that I became impatient at times.

Lettie, the little girl next door, invited me to come over to her house to see a new music box she had received on her birthday.

"Put on a clean apron and you may go," my mother told me.

The apron I was to wear had wide strings that were tied on the shoulders, and immediately I ran to my mother to have her tie them for me.

"But you learned how to tie bows last week," she said as she took a fluffy doughnut out of a pan of hot lard.

"Yes, but I've never put my apron on by myself before," I objected.

"Tying a bow on an apron is done exactly as we tied the one with the ribbon," she said, drawing the pan of lard to the back of the kitchen range and coming over to where I was standing.

I thought she intended to put on my apron, and I handed it to her.

"No, we are going to do this together," she said. "Why don't you try tying the bow first and then putting on the apron?"

I began to struggle with the ties and soon they were wrinkled, and all the starch was out of them. But at last, I succeeded in tying one of the bows all by myself.

"That's right," my mother said, ignoring the limpness of the bow. "Now let us try the other one."

This went much easier.

"1 knew you could do it," my mother told me, patting me on the shoulder. "And now perhaps you'll go upstairs and bring down

your pink apron. I think I would a little rather you wore that over at Helena's house today."

In a minute I returned with the pink apron, which had ties at the shoulders exactly like those on the blue one which I had brought down first.

"Now let us see how well we can tie these bows," my mother said, smiling encouragingly.

I tied both bows on the pink apron without any trouble, and Lettie and I were off to play with the new music box at her house. I didn't need help to put on any of my aprons after that.

Since I had been taught to take care of myself at home, I could play outdoors with other children my own age without being a drag on them. When no one was in sight, I crawled on my hands and knees to get close enough to the ground to see the figures that the children had drawn for a game of hopscotch. Soon I, too, could draw them in the sand, both the oblong figure for regular hopscotch and the one for the game they called snake hopscotch, and it was easy after that to learn to play the games. However, if the ground was too hard the figures were dim and after a long, dry spell I prayed for rain so 1 could see the lines in the sand well enough to throw my hopscotch block where it belonged.

I watched the others jump rope and then I ran home and practiced it by myself. At first, I stumbled and got caught in the rope, and I had some bad falls; but I discovered that singing helped me catch the rhythm of the turning of the rope. I tried jumping in front door and back door, and at last I was ready to join my playmates. However, I found that when someone else turned the rope I couldn't see it quickly enough to hop at the exact second it came down and, since many of the children turned the rope unevenly, I missed all the time. Then I pretended that I preferred to be one of the rope turners and, since no one else cared particularly for this job, I earned considerable popularity because of my seeming preference for it.

I bought the largest jacks that were to be had at the corner candy store and I kept them brightly polished because they could be seen more easily that way. Few of my playmates had such fine jacks and I never lacked a partner for this game. When dominoes were suggested, I waited cautiously to see whether the chips to be used had red or blue or white spots on their black backgrounds. If the spots were red or blue, I said 1 didn't want to play, for I knew I couldn't see well enough to get along at all. If they were white, I had a fine time, even though I could see only the chips closest to me and had to guess at the rest and consequently went to the boneyard so often that I lost the game anyway.

After I had received a pair of shining skates for Christmas, I played with them indoors for weeks before I ventured out of the house. I became familiar with the touch of every part of them and 1 learned to put them on without looking at them. Then I was ready to join the other children on the skating pond on a near-by vacant lot which the firemen at our station had flooded for us. My father built a snow mound in our back yard, and I could steer my sled down this because I knew every bump on it. But I was afraid to try the long, steep hill where the older boys and girls coasted so much that the tracks changed all the time.

I played hide-and-seek, run-sheep-run, prisoner's base, tag, last-couple-out, and other running games with the children in our neighborhood in Minneapolis and I was considered a fairly good runner. We usually played in our back yard or at one of the neighbors' or in the park across the street or on the campus of Augsburg Seminary a block away. I was well acquainted with the grounds at all these places and could have gone over them blindfolded. But if the games were played in less familiar places, I became timid at once and retired into the background and dropped out of the game.

It was at our summer home at Lake Minnetonka that I had most of my fun during my childhood. Our place lay along the lake shore and we children played out of doors from early in the spring until late in the fall. Flowers grew wild everywhere and so did trees and interesting plants. Near the house my father had set out birches, evergreens, oaks, lindens, and American elms. There was an orchard back near the road where apple, plum, and cherry trees grew, and we children feasted on their fruit long before it was ripe. Farther along the south slope was a good-sized grape vineyard and on the flats near the lake were patches of strawberries, raspberries,

blackberries, gooseberries, and currants, and a fine vegetable garden. In the front part of the place green lawns were terraced down to the lake. These were dotted with flower beds in which plants bloomed all summer.

My father taught all of us children to swim. My mother used to say that I could not have been more than two years old when she saw me take my first strokes alone. She may have exaggerated to encourage me, although I became a fairly good swimmer before I was very old. I also learned to manage an oar when my arms were too short to stretch across the width of the boat.

I was taken along several times when the older people in the family went fishing, but I made such a nuisance of myself that I was left at home after that. I think my lack of interest may have been due in part to the fact that I could not see the bob as it floated on top of the water. I was not squeamish about baiting my own hook with either grub or angleworms and I volunteered to do this for others in the boat, but it was discouraging to sit and watch one fine fish after another being pulled in without having the satisfaction of knowing that I was getting as much as a single nibble.

Nor did I take much interest in the little playhouse which had been built at the lake especially for us children. Perhaps this was because I didn't enjoy playing with dolls. Whenever I played in the playhouse, I lived upstairs. This meant sitting perched upon the red roof, which I had reached by swinging myself through the open window and pulling myself up to the lower part of the steep slope on the roof. If I had a ladder, I brought clay with me and a small thin board and I made squares of cheese and butter and fancy layer cakes out of the clay and sold them to the good housekeepers who lived downstairs. On the rare occasions when I stayed downstairs, the place very soon became a schoolroom or a showhouse and my playmates were my pupils or members of my show troupe.

1 also climbed upon the highest branches of the tallest trees. I used to pull off my shoes and stockings to make the going easier, and I learned to recognize every variety of tree by running the soles of my bare feet along their trunks. I had a favorite linden that stood on the brink of the hill overlooking the lake and I often went there to think and to dream.

If my mother ever had any misgivings about my climbing, she did not let me know; for she included the other children whenever she pointed out any particular danger we might encounter in our play. "You will be very careful, will you not?" she urged gently.

I was allowed to play down by the lake shore with the other children, too. Here I spent many happy hours digging in the sand

and wading in the shallow water that skirted the beach. We children dampened the sand so it would stick together, and we patted it into elegant houses on our estates. We put willow twigs into the ground for trees and picked wildflowers up in the hillside for our gardens. Our driveways were lined with snails, and the clams furnished silver seats for us with their shells. We used boards which had been washed ashore for boats, and little stones for passengers and crews. If a high wave washed everyone overboard, we scooped up a fresh supply of the pebbles that blinked in the sunlight under the clear water and started out on another voyage.

Croquet was a favorite pastime among the young people at the lake. By tying white rags on the tops of the arches it was possible for me to play, too, although I usually came out behind the rest. This did not lessen my interest in the game, however, and I played whenever I had the chance; that is, when too many good players were not around to use the balls and mallets. Once in a great while someone volunteered to stand close to the arches when I took my shot, and this seemed to help me more than the white rags. On one such occasion I came out first in the game. Since I never repeated this record, the probabilities are that it was only a streak of freak luck. I didn't get along very well at playing horseshoe, for no matter how carefully I took aim the shoe would not encircle the stick. It was thin and far away, and I didn't seem to be able to gauge my distance properly. I was a total failure at ball—all but at soft ball, when a rhyme was recited to keep time with the bouncing of the ball against the cement:

One, two, buckle my shoe. Three, four, shut the door. Five, six, pick up sticks. Seven, eight, lay them straight.

Despite my mother's careful teaching and my own interest in what was going on around me, it was sometimes difficult for me to coordinate what 1 was actually seeing with what people were talking about, since much of what I learned had to come to me through other channels than my eyes.

I remember distinctly the confusion there was in my mind over the word coffin.

My sister Ruth died when I was about six years old. That was the winter we younger children had measles, whooping cough, and diphtheria. At the time of Ruth's death my sister Esther and I were on the road to recovery, but we were still weak and were downstairs only during the funeral. My father lifted me up so I could see Ruth as she lay in what he in Norwegian called her kiste. Not long afterward Mrs. Wales, the woman next door, also died and her funeral was held from her home. From our sitting room bay window, 1 saw several men carry out something that to me looked like a rolled-up quilt—black with a bright-colored border in it. My sister Olga, who stood beside me told me that was Mrs. Wales's coffin, and that Mrs. Wales was inside of it. There was no connection in my mind be-tween the black quilt 1 thought I was seeing and the white bedlike box in which my sister Ruth had lain. The following year 1 started school. Early in the fall my chum Alma and I were walking home to lunch one noon when Alma said there was a crape on the door of the house we were passing.

"Someone is dead in there," Alma remarked in a grown-up manner, "and there'll be many pretty flowers. Let's go in."

I said I couldn't do that because my mother had forbidden me to go into anyone's house without her permission.

"No one will know the difference," Alma said confidently. "Weil just ask to view the remains. That's what you're supposed to say when you want to look at dead people. We'll come right out again. Come on. They'll have real roses from the greenhouse."

Real roses from the greenhouse. I had never seen any except the one time at Ruth's funeral, and then I wasn't close enough to get a good look at them or to touch them. I weakened and we turned in at the gate. Alma rang the bell, and a middle-aged woman opened the door and ushered us into a large, chilly parlor where the shades were all closely drawn. I clutched Alma's hand as I stumbled over the floral pieces that were draped over tables and chairs and lying on the floor. The heavy scent of the flowers made me dizzy, and I saw dimly in one corner of the room a young lady lying with her hands folded over her breast in a white bedlike box similar to the one in which my sister Ruth had been and which my father had called a kiste.

"She had a real elegant coffin," Alma said calmly as we went down the walk toward the street once more.

I was not at all surprised that I had missed seeing the coffin, but I speculated a good deal about just where in the room it had been. Perhaps it had lain on the floor among the flowers ready to be wrapped around the lady when she was taken out of the house.

After that, Alma and I stopped in at every house where she spied a crape on the door; and of each person who answered our ring we asked permission to view the remains. On these visits we saw a tiny baby who had lived only a few hours after birth; a little boy who Alma said was swollen to almost twice his size, because he had died of dropsy; a consumptive whom the children had called the living skeleton; and the sister of one of the girls in our room, who had been struck down by a streetcar. All these dead people lay in white bedlike boxes surrounded by masses of flowers in chilly, dimly lighted rooms where I held Alma's hand as I made my way about. Each time we were outside again Alma commented on the elegance of the coffin. I wanted to ask her if they were all black with bright-colored borders like the one they carried Mrs. Wales in; but I was afraid Alma would laugh at me for displaying my ignorance, so I didn't.

Then old Mr. Sivertsen died. He was one of our nearest neighbors and of course Alma and I went to view the remains. Mr. Sivertsen was lying in a bedlike box exactly like my sister Ruth's, except that it was black and so large that there were mounds of flowers on the top of it. The shades were partly open in Sivertsens' parlor and the room was fairly light. I knew at once that this was the same kind of black coffin that Mrs. Wales had been conducted in. What I thought had looked like a colored border had in reality been bright-colored flowers. And at last, 1 knew that the word kiste in Norwegian meant the same as coffin in English.

There were other words and expressions that puzzled me; and because I was embarrassed for not knowing what everyone else did, months and sometimes years passed before I learned the real meaning of some of them.

My older brother Oscar went across the lake one evening to meet a guest who was coming out from Minneapolis on the train. It was late, so we waited for dinner until eight o'clock.

"You must be starving," my mother said to the guest when she arrived.

"Not at all," the guest replied cheerfully. "I had some gum on the boat."

I had been in our rowboat hundreds of times, but I had never seen any gum there. This, too, I decided, was something I had missed. Since it was not entirely dark yet, I ran down to the lake shore as fast as I could and climbed eagerly into the boat. I lay down on my stomach and pressed my face against both the sides and the wide centerboard at the bottom, and I passed my hands carefully under the seats and over both oars bring in the stern. I even peeled some of the blistered paint off the bow on the outside of the boat, thinking this might be gum, and put it in my mouth, only to spit it out as soon as I had tasted it I was sure that, no matter how hungry our guest had been, she hadn't eaten that.

I was almost in tears when I gave up my search for gum on the boat. I ran around the hill and climbed it at the back near the road where no one would see me and find out what I had been doing.

Another incident which occurred when I was a very little girl not only confused me but also caused me considerable worry.

A man who lived in the country about a mile from our home was drowned one summer, and people said that although he had been a good swimmer, he had not been able to save himself because he had been drinking. There was much talk about the bad end to which his years of carousing had finally brought him, and I listened with wide-open ears. Among those whom I heard discussing the tragedy was a good but self-righteous neighbor of the dead man.

"I hope Mr. B. saw his sins before he sank under the water for the last time," she said tearfully, "so he had time to repent and be saved."

After the drowning of Mr. B. I looked around stealthily whenever I went bathing to see whether I could find anything that might be one of my sins. A patch of seaweed tangled about my legs under the water startled me, and a stray water lily and a dead fish floating beside me brought out goose pimples all over my body. If only I had an idea of how a sin looked, I thought, it would be easier to spot one.

Because of my limited vision, everything with which I was not familiar frightened me if it came to me without warning. I couldn't take things in at a glance as other children did. That is why I had a mortal fear of cats, while I wasn't at all afraid of dogs.

When a dog approached me, he announced his presence with a bark or a growl or a snarl or a sniff. If on rare occasions he failed to give warning with these signals, his thudding paws or the swishing of his tail told me he was there. Not so the cat. She would slink noiselessly along and then all of a. sudden pounce on me.

Only after she had thoroughly frightened me would she meow or yowl so I could hear her.

My mother tried to rid me of my aversion to cats, insisting that they would not harm me. She petted them to show me how friendly they were, and she begged me to stroke them, too. But I was miserable all the time they were near me, and my mother finally gave up trying to get me to like them.

When my father had a contract to resurvey Hennepin County, Minnesota, he employed a large number of men who lived in camps while the work was being done. One of his rodmen was bitten by a wildcat in the woods and died from hydrophobia soon afterward. I may have heard the older people talk about this sad affair, for it seemed that I was much more afraid of cats after it had happened.

A few years later a practical joker, knowing of my fear, threw a huge cat at me one dark night. I felt its claws dig through my thin dress and into my back and I heard it meow as it crawled up toward my neck. I ran for blocks before anyone could catch me and relieve me of the cat. I had a perfect horror of the animals from then on.

While Uncle Enoch was a medical student at the University of Minnesota and was living at our home, I heard him say one day that he had taken some cats' brains up to his room and that they were preserved in wood alcohol. There was a strong smell from the alcohol, but I thought it was from the cats' brains. A few weeks later when I was running a temperature with a cold, my mother gave me an alcohol rub. That night I had a nightmare and dreamed I saw green cats' eyes glowering at me out of the dark.

Whenever I had nightmares after that, I dreamed of cats. Sometimes they were headless, whirling in dizzy circles above my head, and sometimes they tormented me by coming down and jumping at me.

It was not easy for my mother to keep me as well dressed as the other children in the family, for I played so hard that my clothes were invariably the first ones to wear out. On the night before we moved from the lake, my father had to put paper soles in my shoes so I could wear them into town. This happened no matter how many pairs I had had during the season.

On winter evenings my father knitted on a knitting machine the legs of stockings for all of us children, and an old woman finished off the toes and heels by hand. Several extra pairs of stockings were provided for me, yet long before spring I was stockingless and had to wear ready-made woolen ones until it was warm enough for cotton.

I carried stones and shells and hopscotch blocks and other trinkets around with me and tore big holes in my pockets while my dresses were still new. At last, my mother was reduced to malting sham pockets in my clothes.

All the climbing I did was hard on my clothes, too. The picket fence between our yard and the neighbor's at the lake caused many bad accidents. I used to straddle the pickets instead of walking around to the gates, and the pickets were forever poking through my skirts and tearing large gashes in them. Once I lost my balance and fell and was left hanging by the petticoat. Ragnhild, my playmate, was waiting for me on the other side of the fence and came to my rescue. I was not hurt, but my petticoat was ruined.

When I was old enough, my mother had me clean and press and air my clothes just as my older sisters did. I spent many a Saturday afternoon pressing pleats into my skirts. I was also expected to repair my clothes if I could see to do what was needed; if not, to get someone to help me with what I couldn't do.

"There is no excuse for anyone to be slovenly about his appearance," my mother often remarked.

Long before I could read, I knew many stories from the Scandinavian classics. Mv mother told us the stories of Hans Christian Andersen, Asbjornsen and Moe, and Bjornstjerne Bjornson. The Three Sillies, A Happy Boy, and The Ugly Duckling were my favorites. I am not sure what there was about The Three Sillies that interested me except that it was so ridiculous. I can still hear my mother, while we children were all laughing, finishing the List sentence: "And when the poor man came home, his wife was planting salt." In the story of A Happy Boy, I could sympathize with Oivind be-cause 1 was very fond of food myself. But it was The Ugly Duckling that impressed me the most. The story of the change that came over the Ugly Duckling, making him a beautiful swan, never failed to inspire me with the hope that someday a miracle would happen to me, too, that would change my eyes so I would be like other people.

I also loved to hear mv mother tell us children's true stories about mv grandmother in Norway. My mother made me feel that mv grandmother was a remarkable person and she became a heroine out of the past to me, like Ruth in the Bible and Martha Washington. My mother told us children how my grandmother went into the woods and dug up roots of shrubs that grew wild there; she also picked berries, and from these and the wild roots she made dyes which colored the gray wool from the backs of the sheep into the most beautiful shades of red and blue and green and brown. If a cow went away from the rest of the herd, all my grandmother had to do was to chop into fine pieces a part of the dishcloth belonging to the wife of the neighbor on whose land the cow had strayed, sprinkle a dash of salt on it, say an incantation that only my grandmother knew, and then feed the mixture to the cow; and the cow would immediately return to the herd and follow the bell cow and would never wander off by herself again. (I only realized much later that it was die salt which brought the cow home.) My grandmother also had great power over wolves that skulked about the mountains in Osterdalen, especially during the winter. Even those which swooped down from Finland knew better than to molest any of the sheep that belonged to the flock from the Haugseth estate, no matter how far from home the sheep had wandered. Yet sheep belonging to other farmers nearby would be killed in large numbers and devoured by the wolves.

Once my grandmother saw a real ghost. It was the spirit of a woman who had committed suicide some years earlier. My grandmother became so frightened by the ghost that without thinking she called upon God to protect her, and at this the ghost disappeared. My grandmother regretted afterward that she had not questioned the ghost, for the chances were that its visit to my grandmother had some important purpose.

My grandmother could neither read nor write; yet she could sing every hymn in the Lutheran hymnal no matter how many verses it had, and she knew prayers by heart that were so long that it took half an hour or more to say one of them. Every year she sold one-tenth of the sheep of her herd and her best milk cow and gave the money she received for them to the China mission. She was very interested in foreign lands although she had not been outside the valley in which she lived, and when my mother left for America, my grandmother planned to follow her in a few years. But my grandmother became ill and died, and so she never got to see the outside world.

My father also entertained us children with stories. He generally recited them to us on Sunday mornings when he sat with the youngest on his knee and the rest huddled as close to him as we could get. Most of his tales were in rhyme and he recited them, one after the other, without stopping. One was about a Chinese emperor who melted in his own grease because the sun in China was so hot. Another was about a troll which lived under a waterfall. Still another described the exploits of a great Norwegian king who was killed on his ship, Ormen Lange. And then there was the story about Wise Knute who could see into the future and foretell what was going to happen to people. Because his head had to hold so much wisdom, there was not a hat or a cap in the entire kingdom of Norway big enough for him to wear.

I was only a very little girl when I began to wish for the day when I might visit this fairyland in the far North from which my parents had come.

During those early years I received thorough instruction in religion at home from my mother. She talked about God as though He was someone she knew very well, and she made us children have the same feeling toward Him. Would God like this? Would He be angry at that? We came to my mother with such questions constantly. She told us stories from the Bible every evening when she put us to bed and the one who was first to be undressed had the privilege of naming which story it was to be. My mother told these stories in such simple language and so vividly that I had definite pictures in my mind of all the people and I was sure that, even though I couldn't see very well, I would recognize them in heaven if I ever got there myself.

After we children had all settled down for the night my mother always prayed aloud. She sat with bowed head and folded hands near the crib of the youngest of us and she spoke in a low, dear voice so we could all hear. I used to peek through my own folded hands to look at her because I thought she was so beautiful. She wore fine checked black and white house dresses with stiff cuffs and a crisp white collar fastened in front with a large gold pin, and a white, spotless apron that tied at the waist. Sometimes she just made up the prayers and then she put into them anything special she wanted to say to God. In these prayers of her own making, she often mentioned me and asked God to please let me see well enough so I could live a useful and happy life and do the work He had planned for me. I can't remember being especially moved by these petitions, for she spoke so quietly and confidently that it seemed as natural for her to be asking this for me as it was for her to pray for other things my siblings needed. Sometimes my mother repeated one of the long prayers she had learned from her mother and then we children listened very closely, for these prayers were almost as interesting as the fairy tales or the true stories about my grandmother in Norway.

When we were all so sleepy that we could only half pronounce the words, we repeated together the prayer my mother had taught us: Now I close my eyes, O Father on high. Take me into Thy safekeeping. From sin, from sorrow, from danger, Thy angel protect me Who hath guided my footsteps today. Amen.

Our prayers and our religious instruction were all in Norwegian and I was under the impression that that was God's own language. My mother taught us to read Norwegian before we started public school so we could study our Sunday school lessons in our Norwegian books. She told me, after I was older, that she worried for fear I didn't see well enough to be able to read and she waited longer than with the others to begin my Norwegian lessons.

One day she decided she couldn't postpone trying to teach me any longer. She brought out a little book with brown cardboard covers from the shelf in the corner and taking me by the hand, led me to the wicker rocker at the sitting room bay window, where we sat down together. Then she opened the link brown book to the first page.

"I wonder how well you can see these letters?" she asked me as she raised the book toward me.

1 took it in both hands and buried my face in it, flattening my nose against its pages so that the eye with which I could see was directly below the first letter. Then I tipped the book into an oblique position, bringing the letter still closer to me and at an angle where the light could shine on it.

"That is A," 1 said after I had gotten myself adjusted.

"Good," my mother said encouragingly, "Can you tell me what the next one is?"

"That is B," I said.

"Go on," my mother said.

"C-D-E-F-G," I read, moving my head as I pronounced each letter.

At the end of the line, I moved my head toward the left of the page once more and fixed my eye just below the second row of letters. I continued in this way until I had gone over the entire alphabet. My nose never left the paper except when I shifted fines.

"You have committed to memory the alphabet beautifully," my mother said, taking the book from me, "but now we must really try to recognize each letter when we see it on the page. Take the book and say aloud the letters of that first word you see."

Again, I grasped the book and buried my face in it. There was a picture of a boy feeding a bone to a dog that was sitting up begging for it, and a cat dangling a mouse in its paws. Without stopping to spell out the words I began to read the short sentences that were printed under each picture. I became so interested that I didn't stop until I had finished the page.

"What does the book say about this boy?" my mother asked in a low voice as she pointed to a page farther on where there was a picture of a boy falling out of a tree.

I read about a naughty boy who had skipped school and run away from home and gone to the woods. After I had stopped and she didn't say what to do next, I looked up inquiringly at her. Something wet fell on my cheek and my mother took out her handkerchief and wiped it and her own.

"And this?" she asked.

It was the story of a little girl named Emma who wouldn't eat the soup her mother had cooked for dinner because Emma said she didn't like it. The following day Emma ate heartily, and her mother said it was the same soup. This time Emma was hungry. Everything tasted good when one was hungry, her mother said.

"I believe you are really seeing what you are reading," my mother said, smiling.

Without waiting for her to take the book from me this time, I turned the leaves until I came to the picture of a family gathered around a Christmas tree. Burying my face once more, I read what was on the opposite page.

"That is wonderful, dear," mv mother said, taking me in her arms and kissing me. "To think I was afraid you couldn't see well enough to read."

She let me down from her lap and then went over to the bookshelf and brought back with her an even smaller book than the one we had just been reading.

"We'll start right out in the Catechism," she said, a glad ring in her voice. "And now let us see what we can do with the first commandment."

My mother often said she wondered when I had learned to read Norwegian without being taught. She thought perhaps I had listened to the older children and gotten it in that way. I myself have no recollection of how it happened.

Most of our instruction in Sunday school consisted of committing to memory the entire contents of the Catechism, the Book of Explanations, the Bible History, long passages from the Bible itself, and church hymns. This method of teaching was wonderful for me because it provided an excellent drill in accurate memorizing, which I have had need of every day of my life.

My mother had a rather ingenious system of teaching the girls in the family how to do housework. She divided the household tasks into groups according to the skill needed to perform them, and the youngest one of us started out with the simplest one.

My first job consisted of scrubbing the chairs in our kitchen at the lake. I had been waiting for weeks to hear my mother say I was old enough to do this; so, when one Saturday morning she announced at the breakfast table that I was to begin that day, I was jubilant.

She brought the chairs and a pan of lukewarm water out on the grass for me, and then she showed me exactly how to go about bolding the scrub brush and the rag in order to scrub the chairs properly. Although she did most of the actual work, she praised me for the good beginning I had made, and she left the chairs and my apron and me out in the sun to dry.

Soon I was ready to take on another job. This one was much more important, and I was very proud to be entrusted with it. It consisted of the regular weekly cleaning of the outside toilet at our home at the lake. My mother was most particular about how this was to be done. First the ceiling and the walls and the floor and everything else in there had to be scrubbed thoroughly with hot soapsuds applied with a long, stiff broom. Then several pailfuls of cold, clear water dashed into the place, and the stiff broom applied once more for the rinsing. After that evergreen boughs had to be cut off the scrubbiest trees. Some of them were broken up into rather large pieces and hung on the toilet walls on nails especially driven in for that purpose. The rest of the evergreen was torn into tiny shreds and strewn over the newly scrubbed floor. Last of all, newspapers had to be cut into uniform-sized sheets just large enough to fit into the box in one corner of the floor. At first, I carried out my mother's instructions to the letter, but when the newness had worn off, I became careless and threw large, gnarled sticks on the floor and jammed the newspapers into the box without bothering to cut them. My mother talked to me severely about this.

"Do you mean to tell me that, after you have shown me how well you can see to work, you are satisfied to leave the toilet looking as it does? You cannot expect me to be proud of you when you disappoint me like this."

The scrubbing of the cellar stairs at the lake was a distinct promotion from the job on the toilet. The only approach to the cellar was from a trap door in the corner of the kitchen floor, and at first my mother opened this for me. She also warned me about being careful to keep my balance while I was working and she showed me how to wipe the ledges into which the trap door fitted, so no dirt would fall into the cellar. It was most important of all; however, she told me, that I should wipe the steps absolutely dry; otherwise, someone might slip and fall.

"If I did not know how careful you are," she said to me, "I would not have you wash the cellar steps. But 1 am sure you will do it well."

I wiped every step until it was almost as dry as if it hadn't been washed at all, for I felt as though the lives of the entire family were in my safekeeping.

Later, I helped with the work in our city home in Minneapolis. Here the woodwork and the floors were dark and highly polished, and the slightest trace of dust showed up on them.

"You can do better than that," my mother would tell me, taking me by the hand and pointing out the places I had missed. "We who are not able to see as well as the others must take more pains with our work. When we show how well we can get along, no one will remember that we have trouble with our eves."

As I grew older, I was permitted to help with the washing and the ironing. My father usually got up early the morning of washday and turned the washing machine before he left for the office. I learned first how to rinse clothes and to hang them on the line. Sometimes I had to take them down and rehang them several times before they suited my mother.

"It doesn't matter how they look on the line," I complained, "just so they dry."

"That is exactly why they have to be hung so carefully," my mother reminded me. "They won't dry properly if they are bunched up. Besides, there is a right and a wrong way of doing everything. And you want to know how to do things the right way, don't you?"

With the ironing my mother was even more exacting.

All our best summer dresses were white and with these we girls wore mounds of starched white underwear. My brothers had white Sunday blouses and my father wore white shirts and light vests. Consequently, our weekly washings, especially at the lake, were prodigious affairs that took two people to do them, standing all day, from four or five in the morning until dinnertime in the evening, in the heat of the kitchen wood stove, on which we heated the flatirons. No matter what else came up, the ironing had to be finished in one day because my mother objected to what she termed "dragging the wash out all week."

In spite of her best efforts, however, my mother didn't succeed in making a seamstress out of me. Since totally blind people do beautiful handwork, my eyes could scarcely be blamed for this. The fact was, most likely, that I lacked patience.

"Why do you bother the youngster with such tomfoolery?" my father asked my mother in my hearing.

"That is no way to talk," my mother said, more sharply than was usual with her. "It isn't kind to let her grow up without teaching her everything the other children can do. What will become of her when I am gone if she doesn't learn to depend upon herself?"

Chapter 2

When I was about five years old, I begged my father and mother to let me go to kindergarten. Alma, my chum, had already stirred and so had Hattie, whose father was the minister of the Baptist church.

My father didn't favor the idea,

"There'll be plenty of time for her to sit poring over books When she begins to go to public school," he told my mother. "Besides didn't you say she is already reading Norwegian out of the Catechism? That is enough for a while."

"She won't sit poring over books at kindergarten," my mother said quietly. "The children really do nothing but play there. It will help her to get used to a routine and to have someone but me teach her. I have heard that Miss Smith and Miss Bailey. her assistant, are both fine women. It wouldn't do any harm to let her try and see how she gets along."

I loved going to kindergarten. The children played the same running games there that I was already used to, but it was much easier for me in kindergarten because there was a circle, marked with a heavy yellow line on the smooth floor, which showed exactly where we were to keep ourselves in the game. In the middle of the forenoon we had a picnic, indoors when it was cold and stormy and on the church lawn on pleasant days. We pasted colored squares and circles of shining paper on cardboard, and I always chose the purple and gold ones because they were so nice and bright.

One morning when Alma came to call me, she said, "We're going to play hooky today."

I didn't know what that was, but it sounded interesting and 1 agreed at once to try it. We stayed out of doors until we were tired, and then I went home. My father was in the yard. He was wearing his high boots and corduroy trousers and short sheepskin coat just as he did when he came home in the evenings after he had been surveying all day.

"Is it going to be night soon?" I asked, running toward him and trying to help him carry the tripod.

"Why no, not for a long time. I just happened to be surveying a lot on Franklin Avenue," he said, lowering the tripod so I could reach it. "But how does it happen that you aren't at kindergarten?"

"Oh," I said happily, "Alma and I are playing a new kind of game today. It's called hooky. It's lots of fun."

My father put the tripod on the porch, and then he sat down on the steps and drew me toward him.

"You must never play hooky again," he said kindly but firmly. "That means you have skipped school. I was afraid when you begged to go to kindergarten that you weren't old enough. But you told me you were a big girl and could do what the other children did. Now you must show me that you can. In our house we always finish what we set out to do."

At the end of the year, we children in the kindergarten had a picnic at Minnehaha Park. My mother sent a box of lunch with me, and I had a nickel tied in my handkerchief to pay for a ride on one of the ponies. I could scarcely wait to show Alma and Hattie the new hat which my mother had trimmed for me. It was a golden-brown straw with a rippled brim and a wreath of blue forget-me-nots around the crown.

We had a wonderful time at the picnic, but when we were ready to go home, I could not find my hat. Miss Smith and Miss Bailey and the other children helped me to hunt for it, but it was nowhere to be seen. It was beginning to look as though I should have to leave without it when Miss Bailey spied it hanging on the top of one of the tallest trees in the park. A soldier in a blue uniform and gold buttons brought it down for me.

"How do you suppose it got up there?" Miss Smith asked wonderingly.

I hung my head. Although I could not be sure that this was the particular tree I had climbed during the morning, and I had no recollection of leaving my hat on one of its branches while I was up there, I knew I had chosen the tallest tree I could End.

I was very happy riding home on the streetcar with my hat perched safely on the top of my head.

I looked forward to attending public school even more than I had kindergarten. The public school, or big school as we children in kindergarten called it, continued through both the morning and the afternoon, and at the end of the day those who went there came home looking important with their arms full of books and papers. Ellen and Olga, my two older sisters, and my older brother Oscar all attended public school and I had heard from them what a wonderful place it was. Exciting bells rang every once in a while, and the teachers put up pictures all around the room and wrote interesting things on the blackboard for the children to copy. And the children read English out of books with colored pictures— instead of Norwegian, which anyone could learn without going to school at all.

All summer I counted the hours for school to begin.

Then the great day came. I got up when it was still dark and put on my brand-new pair of brown slippers with gold buckles on them which my father had brought out from town for me the night before, and the new red jumper dress with the white guimpe my mother had just finished.

When we children arrived at the school building, my sister Ellen showed me my room; but I told her she need not go with me any farther, for I could take care of myself.

I walked confidently into the room and over to the teacher, who was sitting just inside the door at her desk. She did not look up but continued with some writing she was doing.

"My name is Borghild Margarethe Dahl," I told her.

"What?" she asked, still writing.

"My name is Borghild Margarethe Dahl," I repeated. "Will you please spell it?" she asked, looking up at last.

I did, just as my mother had taught me.

The teacher frowned and said something I couldn't quite understand about outlandish names of foreigners. Her gaze, which she now fixed on me, made me uneasy.

"Tell me," she asked after a while, "what do you see on that blackboard over there?"

I said I couldn't see anything.

"Then what are you doing here?" she demanded. "This isn't a school for the blind. We don't take children here who can't see."

Not to be taken to a big school? That couldn't be, I told myself in a sudden panic.

The teacher continued to sit regarding me closely.

I tried to think what I should do. I wasn't blind. I could see. Not as well as the rest of the children, but my mother let me help do everything at home just like the others, and she said that when we did our work well no one would notice anything about our eyes.

I couldn't go home. My father had told me that we always finished what we started in our house. I would have to make the teacher understand that I could see.

"I can see," I said, "only not so far away."

Still, she continued to regard me in a manner that was anything but reassuring.

I became desperate. How could I convince her that I was not blind? That I was actually seeing her, and the children around me who had come into the room while I had been standing there? One little girl, tugging at her mother's skirts, was in tears. I was almost crying myself, but I knew that if I did cry, I would spoil my chances of being permitted to star.

And, come what may, I had made up my mind that I was going to stay at school.

Then, like a flash, a happy thought came to me. I was so pleased about it that I ran over to the other side of the teacher's desk and grasped her arm.

"Oh, Miss A," I exclaimed (I had heard her name dozens of times from the older children), "I can see! And I can see your wart, too, right on the top of your nose."

I can't remember what she said to this; but it must have convinced her that I could see, for I know I was permitted to stay.

When I went out at recess that morning, I looked for Alma and Hattie. But I couldn't find them or anyone else I knew. I walked about the school grounds peering into the faces of the children near me to see whether I could recognize any of them. I went right up close to several who I thought might be some of my friends, but in each case, I found that I was mistaken. Then a little way off near the fence I thought I saw Richard, a boy living in our neighborhood. I ran over to him.

"Oh, Richard," I cried, "what is your teacher's name? Mine is Miss A."

The boy stared at me blankly and then he began to giggle.

"Look, kids," he called to some boys standing at a little distance from him. "Look what's come to school."

The boys sauntered over to me, and after they had taken one good look at me, they burst into a chorus of guffaws.

"Blind pig," one of them said, loud enough for everyone around me to hear.

"Bullhead," another one yelled.

"Gee for a sight," came from a third one.

The same boys singled me out when I went home to lunch and when I returned for the afternoon session. They were also waiting for me at the beginning of the afternoon recess period. Each time they saw me they ran after me, calling me names that were suggestive of my appearance, especially my eyes. When school was over for the day, I tore all the way home and into the house to get away from them. No one was there. I rushed upstairs and into my mother's bedroom. I grasped the hand mirror from her dresser and ran up the stairs into the attic. I went over to the west window, where the sun was pouring in, and I pressed the mirror flat against my face. For the first time in my life, I was able to see exactly how I looked.

One of my eyes was much smaller than the other because it had sunk far back into my head. It was all one dead, gray blue mass and much lighter than the other one. I stared at my reflection, and I could see after a while that even the good eye had a white spot in the blue part of it. I also noticed that the lid of the poor eye remained partly closed. First, I tried to open it wide like the other one, and when I found that I couldn't do this I held the lid open with my fingers. This hurt me so much that I had to drop my eyelids. Then, shutting both eyes, I tried to look at myself, but I couldn't manage that at all. With both eyes closed, I thought I would look like other people. If only people could see me while I was sleeping! I lay down on the floor and closed my eyes and pretended I was fast asleep.

After I had opened my eyes once more, I took another long look at myself. At the full realization of how I must appear to other people, I burst into tears.

At home I had never been made to feel that my eyes affected my appearance in any way. My sister Esther, who was very beautiful, and I were usually dressed alike, and my mother planned my clothes with as much care as those of the other children. For my last birthday she had made me a sky-blue woolen dress with gilt buttons and yellow featherstitching on it, and I called it my gold dress. But now, I thought, with my eyes, even though I wore my gold dress, I couldn't be beautiful like the other children.

The following morning the boys were out on the playground when I came to school. Since I knew how terrible I must appear to them, their taunts hurt me more than ever. I ran past them and into the school building; but a teacher stood just inside the door, and she stopped me before I had gotten more than a few feet beyond it.

"Go right out again," she commanded. "Don't you know that you are not supposed to come in before the last bell rings I found a basement entrance and I slipped through that and succeeded in reaching my room without meeting anyone. But my own teacher met me at the door there.

"Borgull," she said sternly, "if you want to stay in school, you will have to learn to obey the rules here. Go right out and play with the other children until the last bell rings."

At noon that day I stayed at home until I was sure the boys would have gone into the schoolhouse. Then I started off, running as fast as I could. I wasn't bothered this time, for the grounds were entirely deserted. But when I reached my room, my teacher scolded me before all my classmates for being tardy.

My father took us the children for the week end out to the lake and I told my mother about the boys at school. With tears streaming down her cheeks, she begged me not to mind them. They didn't understand what they were doing, she said, or they wouldn't talk like that. If I pretended that I didn't notice them, she was sure they would soon stop.

Perhaps what my mother said was true. Perhaps the boys in my room took my part against the other boys, for I soon became very friendly with all my schoolmates. Or the teachers may have heard about my predicament and have done something about it. After that first week I did not suffer any more humiliation from the boys, nor can I remember that I was ever bothered by other children on the school grounds after that. Whenever I was taunted about my eyes it was by strangers, and those did not continue with it for long if the children who knew me were within hearing distance. I never told my mother when this happened. I think, after that first time, I realized how much it hurt her to hear about it, and I had a feeling that it would not be right to go to her—without being able to take it on the chin by myself.

My experience with my primary teacher that first day of school and the taunts from the boys during the week which followed left scars on my memory which time was never really able to erase. Sometimes the feeling came over me that I had no right to live and that I was guilty of something— I didn't know just what—when people were kind to me and treated me as if I were one of them.

One of the things at school of which I had heard a great deal was what the older children called tests. They talked about the tests in a half-fearful, half-boastful manner and I

was very curious to find out what they were like. When, therefore, our second-grade teacher announced one day that we were to have a test in language the following afternoon, I waited for this new experience with my usual eager impatience.

At last, the day for the test came. It was the last period before dismissal. We children were all ready with carefully sharpened pencils in our hands and sheets of rough, gray, blue-lined paper on our desks before us.

"Remember," our teacher told us as she stood in front of us at the blackboard, "you must not give any help to anyone nor receive any while you are writing this test. If you do, you will be cheating, and I shall have to throw your papers into the wastebasket and give you zero in the test. That will mean that you will not pass at the end of the term."

I did not dare to turn to the right nor to the left for fear the teacher would think I was copying from those around me and would throw my paper into the wastebasket for cheating. But though I looked straight ahead at the blackboard where she was writing the questions and strained my eye so hard trying to see that everything around me became blurred, I could not make out a single word of the examination questions.

I heard pencils scratching and, without turning, I could see dimly Thelma's head on one side of me and Richard's on the other as they bent over their work. The teacher laid down her crayon and turned around toward us children. I bowed my head like the rest and pretended to be writing, too; but then it came to me that my teacher would know that I had been deceiving her as soon as she looked at my paper, and I realized how foolish this was.

I envied Thelma as I heard her pencil race over her paper. She couldn't remember anything outside of school, but she certainly managed to think up a lot to tell the teacher in a test. And she knew what the questions were, so everything she wrote would be all right. I thought of walking up to the board so I could see the questions, too; but if looking around was cheating, walking up to the board must be much worse. I heard the teacher at the back of the room. She cleared her throat, and it sounded so threatening that I decided not to take such a chance.

I was thoroughly miserable. Not being able to pass at the end of the term was, in my opinion, the worst disgrace that could happen to anyone. Two of the boys in my room last year had failed to pass, and I knew I should never be able to survive such humiliation as they must have suffered. The period was nearly over, and soon it would be too late to do anything about seeing the questions on the board.

At last, I mustered all the courage I had and made my way down the aisle back to where the teacher was standing.

"Why, Borgull," she exclaimed after I had told her of my difficulty, "you should have told me at once that you couldn't see the questions. I forgot all about you. Hurry now, or you won't finish. The period is almost over."

She came back to my seat with me and dictated the questions. Then I wrote like mad, my pencil scratching louder than any of the others. When the bell rang, I was just finishing the last question and I was able to hand in my paper with the rest.

I dreaded examinations all through the grades. In crowded rooms it wasn't easy for teachers to remember that I couldn't see boards, and it embarrassed me to have to remind them of it. Some of the teachers always had the questions ready for me on a sheet of paper at the beginning of the period, and I loved these women for their thoughtfulness.

The daily work on the boards did not bother me. My schoolmates were very kind about letting me copy the questions for our lessons, or anything else I had to have, from their papers, or if this was not convenient, I could slip into my schoolroom either early before the teacher had arrived or in the evening after she had gone. Then I could stand right up to the board and, fixing my eye on the word I was copying, I could move right along, walking back and forth in front of the space on the blackboard where the writing was, much in the same manner that I moved my head back and forth over the printed page.

In the fifth-grade things became much easier for me at school. My teacher, Miss Grace Sherwood, knew our family because the older children had been in her room. She realized how little I could see, and she did all she could to help me. We became great friends and I got into the habit of staying after school and visiting with her.

We soon discovered that we had something very much in common. My brother Robert was born that winter and Miss Sherwood had a brand-new niece. We exchanged stories about these two babies, and we told each other about the progress each was making.

"Our baby smiled this morning when my mother was bathing him," I told Miss Sherwood one day.

"My niece knew me last night," she said a few weeks later. "Imagine a baby knowing her aunt when she isn't even three months old. I'm going to spend my whole vacation taking care of her."

Tint summer while we were at the lake, I sat for hours rocking the baby and fanning him as he lay under the mosquito netting in his cradle. I didn't mind what game was interrupted when my mother called me to come in to do this, for I knew that my beloved Miss Sherwood was rocking and fanning her niece, too, and it made me feel very important to be doing exactly the same thing she was.

In the sixth grade my good fortune came right along with me. Miss Everhart, my teacher there, was from the South and she was as gentle and soft-spoken as her Southern dialect.

We studied United States history in her room, and she dwelt on the Civil War for weeks. She told us children that her father had been killed while fighting in the Confederate Army and she cried when she said this. We felt sorry for her even though we had learned earlier that the South had been in the wrong because they had wanted to break up the Union and had Negro slaves. On Decoration Day two soldiers from Fort Snelling came to speak to us children at school and told us about their experiences while they had been fighting on the side of the North. Miss Everhart treated these white-haired men in blue uniforms trimmed with gilt braid and buttons as kindly as though they had been on the same side as her father.

That Decoration Day was an especially happy occasion for me because Miss Everhart had asked me to recite the Gettysburg Address at the program and afterward, she came over and talked to me about it.

"You recited the speech very well," she told me. "I am sure that Lincoln himself could not have put more feeling into it than you did this afternoon."

Miss Everhart was right in thinking that I had been greatly moved while giving the address, for it was one of the rare opportunities I had to take part in anything at school. When children were to represent the room in the lower grades, attractive little girls, or at least those whose eyes did not look like mine, were chosen. I was not called upon to be an angel in the Christmas pageant the year that was given, nor a fairy in the school tableau, nor a soldier in the patriotic drill on Decoration Day, nor a doll in the dress parade, nor a flower in the human bouquet on Arbor Day. When some of the children were sent downtown to the main library, I was one of those who came to school as usual to work at my lessons, pretending not to notice the empty scats of those who had been fortunate enough to be invited to attend the city-wide celebration.

During the presentation of Cinderella, I stood off stage holding the heroine's heavy boots while she danced in her glass slippers out in front. But I listened to the lines of all the actors and actresses and soon afterward put on the play in our barn, coaching the children in our neighborhood for their parts.

Because of overcrowded conditions in our school, the seventh-grade pupils were transferred to other buildings to finish the last two years of grammar school. I had more than a mile to walk to school after that, and it was too far to come home for lunch. I was frightened in my new surroundings, and everything went wrong from the start. It was the fall my brother Robert fad typhoid, and we other children were more or less left to shift for ourselves.

My new teacher and I didn't understand each other. It was more my fault than hers, I know; but I was afraid of her, and I would not tell her I couldn't see the blackboards. I also lacked the courage to Jet her or any of my schoolmates know how close I had to hold books and papers in order to read them. Soon I was regarded by both the teacher and the rest of the pupils as the dunce of the room.

One day we were having The Courtship of Miles Standish in our reading class and the teacher called upon me to recite. I said I didn't know where the place was. She pointed it out to me, but I didn't begin to read. She asked me to stand up, which I did; but I remained dumb.

"I am waiting," the teacher said.

There was no response from me.

"Do you mean to say that you have reached the seventh grade and are unable to read?" she asked sharply.

I felt my cheeks grow hot, and the seats in the room and the heads above them began to swim around me. I knew that, even though I glued my eye to the page now, I should not be able to see a word. Some of the boys started tittering.

"Repeat after me what I say," the teacher commanded. " 'You, John Alden, my friend.' "

By this time, I could neither swallow nor make a sound come out of my throat.

"I am not sure whether you are sullen, or you don't know how to read," the teacher said in disgust. "I'm inclined to think both."

At the end of the first month, I brought home a report card that was full of red marks, indicating that I had failed entirely in my work at school. My older sister Olga went to see the teacher, and the teacher told Olga that my behavior led her to believe that I was not too bright. Olga tried to explain that my vision was extremely poor and that it was therefore hard for me to change schools. The teacher expressed regret at what she termed an additional affliction, but she still maintained her opinion that I was mentally deficient.

After Olga's visit to school my work began to get better. My younger brother Robert recovered from his illness and my mother was able to give the rest of us children more of her attention. At the end of the term, I was promoted and sent into another room, where I had a different teacher. She realized my difficulty at once and we got along well together.

Through one of those strange tricks of fate of which the world is so full, the teacher who found me mentally deficient became years later one of the members of the faculty in the high school of which I was the principal.

In Seven A I sat in front of a boy named Anders Carlson. Anders stuttered and he was passionately fond of art. He did not care for anything else at school, however, and he was continually watching the teacher so she wouldn't catch him drawing when he should have been doing something else. Art was my poorest subject, and I was fascinated by Anders's talent which made it possible for him by a few seemingly careless strokes to produce such beautiful pictures.

In the spring our room did book jackets in watercolor. My attempt in this project was worse than Anders's work in geography and history. To Anders, however, the assignment became a matter of life and death. He became so engrossed in it that he didn't even bother to try to conceal from the teacher that he was working on it all the time, and the understanding teacher let him go on with it without scolding him.

Anders was copying the jacket of the new book Mrs. Wiggs of the Cabbage Patch by Alice Hegan Rice. I watched him from the start and my interest in his painting was almost as keen as his. There was to be an exhibit of the artwork of the entire school, and everyone expected Anders to win the prize.

The afternoon of the last day, when everything was to be sent to the principal's office, both Anders and I stayed after school. I was copying an assignment in geography for the next day, and Anders was, as usual, drawing. After I had finished and had my books out ready to go home, Anders was still working on his book jacket. As I turned around to take one last look at it, I didn't notice that his water pan was close up against the ledge of his desk. I pushed back my elbow, and then I heard the round tin roll down the full length of Anders's desk and plunk first on his seat and afterward down on the floor. There was also a sickening dripping of water.

My insides got all tangled up when I realized the full extent of the damage that had been done to Anders's book jacket. Mrs. Wiggs's cabbage patch had melted into a streaked confusion of colors and the whole drawing was spoiled.

At last, I dared to look at Anders. I saw he was greatly changed. His pale face, instead of being smooth and having a rather vacant expression in it, now was red and drawn and fierce. Even his neck was a deep scarlet, and his clenched fist was slowly moving toward my end of the seat.

"Ya-ya-ya-ya-ya. Da-da-da-da-da-da."

That was as far as he could get. The lining of his white hair went red, too, with the effort he put forth trying to tell me what he thought of me.

I sat perfectly still. My parched throat ached, and my eyes burned. "I know just what you want to say to me, and I don't blame you, Anders," I heard myself saying after a little. "But don't bother to try to talk. It will just make you feel worse. Like when I want to see things so badly and can't."

All at once my eye wasn't dry and neither was my throat.

The angry expression left Anders's face. His naturally pale blue eyes became deep and serene like an October sky.

"Aw-aw-aw. Shu-shu-shucks. Dot-do don't ca-care, B-B-Borghild. It's-s-s all ri-right," he managed to say.

I knew that Anders would never again have anyone who could love him as I did that afternoon.

I changed teachers at the end of the first semester in the eighth grade just as I did in the seventh. I had Miss Cox in Eight B and Miss O'Hearn in Eight A.

Miss Cox was an elderly lady who reminded me of the pictures of Queen Victoria. She was regal in her manner as well as in her appearance, and everyone in the room—even the unruliest boys—stood in awe of her. But she was land, too, and I loved her from the start. During the term an incident occurred which greatly increased my affection for her.

I was absent from school one day; and when I returned, the girls gathered around me and began calling me the teacher's pet.

"Why do you call me that?" I asked.

Then they told me. When Miss Cox, calling the roll found that I was not in my seat, she said she knew that something important must be keeping me away from school because I was so conscientious; but even more than my punctuality and industry, she admired my courage in striving to overcome the handicap of my eyes. And she told the children she was proud to be my teacher. I wouldn't believe at first what the girls told me, but they all insisted that it was true. I couldn't understand how any teacher could be proud of having a girl as ugly looking as I was for a pupil. But the praise warmed my heart and made me try harder than ever to forge ahead.

Miss O'Hearn, my teacher during the second semester, loved literature more than any other subject she taught us and, because she loved it, she made us appreciate it, too. We became familiar with the stories of several classics, and she explained their meaning in such simple language that it was easy to follow what she said. We studied Julius Caesar and, while we were doing it, we dramatized parts of it and memorized long passages from it.

Miss O'Hearn invited Dr. J. S. Montgomery, who had been at Stratford on Avon, to come to speak to us and I shall never forget the impression his talk made upon me. It was the only time anyone with firsthand information about what I had been studying at school spoke of what he had actually seen and heard. I had seen President McKinley when he rode in the Victory Parade in Minneapolis at the end of the Spanish-American War, but not even a President was as important to us children just then as one who had breathed the air around Stratford on Avon and walked the old streets and been in the house where Shakespeare had lived with Anne Hathaway and their three children.

Miss O'Hearn also encouraged us to do silent reading outside of school, and she mentioned books that she thought we might enjoy. Except for the Scandinavian classics which our parents had brought to us children at home, this was the first real direction I had been given in reading. There was a branch library not far from our house; but it was hard for me to see well enough to pick out books there, and the librarian, who was not fond of children, offered no help.

During the summer I read all the books I could lay my hands on—those my friends in the city let me take with me to the lake and, after I had devoured these, whatever I was able to collect in the near-by farmhouses. Modern advisers on juvenile reading would hardly have approved of many of the books I secured in this way—the works of Bertha Clay, Augusta Evans, Marie Corelli, and others like them were in the collection—but I don't know of any particular harm the books did me and I became acquainted with many worthwhile authors.

With constant practice I became a fairly swift reader. Books that were too large for me to hold on my lap, I put on the floor and read crouching doubled over them. Smaller ones which were too unwieldly to handle with comfort, like our geographies at school, I had to dive into, and it was hard for me even then to make out what was on that part of the page which was toward the center of the book. Fine print gave me the most trouble, because I had to study over each word so long that it took a lot of concentration to make any headway reading it.

When I was a very little girl, I used to sing a great deal, but after a siege of diphtheria I lost my voice completely for a while. When it returned, it was hoarse, and I couldn't sing any more. So, I climbed up on the piano stool and picked out on the keys with one finger the tunes of the songs I used to sing.

When I was nine years old, I began to take piano lessons.

I couldn't read the music unless I brought my eye close up to the sheet that stood in front of me, and I had to move my eye from each measure I played. To help me with my practicing, I made up a system of my own. First, I fixed a few notes in my mind and then I learned how to play these on the keyboard of the piano. I committed to memory the rests and the correct fingering in the same way. Then I tried to remember the whole measure, and when I had done this, I began working on the next one. I kept on until I knew the entire line by heart. As soon as I had picked out the melody it was easier, because then I could guess the chords that should go with it, and I recognized variations of this melody every time it was repeated in the piece I was learning.

I had to go back to work on the more difficult parts so I could play them clean. Grace notes were bad because they were so small that, even though my eye was pressed close against the music, I sometimes missed them. Professor Heinrich Gunnarson, my music teacher for many years, was very strict with me and he did a great deal for me by demanding that I play everything I attempted with meticulous correctness.

Because I had to memorize everything I played, my progress on the piano was for a while very slow. But eventually I trained my ear and exercised my fingers so that I could play simple pieces after I had gone over them only a few times. And I accumulated a considerable repertoire for which I needed no sheet music.

The spring I finished the eighth grade, I played in my first piano recital. My piece was Mendelssohn's "Midsummer Night's Dream" suite, and I was listed as Professor Gunnar-son's most advanced pupil.

During that same school year two other events took place which in later years came to have a great influence on my life.

The first was the birth of my youngest sister. She was a fussy baby, but after she was older and easier to manage, I took care of her and played with her whenever I was at home. I loved her more than anyone else in the world.

The second event was my preparation for confirmation. Our minister was a plain, sincere man who took great pains to explain the teachings of Christ to us young people. His faith was so strong that he inspired us to believe, too, that no matter what happened to us there was One Who always directed our lives and helped us when we needed it most. My eyes did not seem nearly so bad after I had listened to him talk to us.

At the church service when I was confirmed, my baby sister was christened. She was given the name of Dorothy Evelyn.

The teacher who registered me for my first semester's work at high school told me that freehand drawing was compulsory for all freshmen.

"Oh, but I can't take that," I objected. "I can't draw. Really I can't."

The teacher smiled.

"Don't you think this an excellent opportunity to learn?" she asked. "After all, that is what schools are for."

My heart sank when I went to class the first day. The instructor was both capable and kind, and the rest of the students started out beautifully. But not I. The teacher gave me extra help, but my work grew, if anything, worse—at least it seemed worse in comparison with what the rest of the class was doing. At last, the teacher called me to her desk.

"You have no artistic sense," she told me. "Proportion; line, color—they evidently mean nothing to you."

She had been so kind to me that I was not at all hurt at what she said. Moreover, I agreed with her that I was no artist. But I would not tell her what I suspected was at least a part of my difficulty—that I couldn't see well enough to draw. If I went up close to the models, I lost my sense of perspective; and if I tried to look at them from a distance, they were blurred and shapeless.

I decided that I would go to Mr. Ozias, our high school principal, and ask his advice.

"Mr. Ozias, I am failing in freshman drawing," I told him. "I'm the worst drawer in South High. Drawing is required for graduation. My parents want me to graduate. What shall I do?"

Mr. Ozias laughed.

" 'Dog won't bite pig. Pig won't jump over the stile, and I shall not get home tonight.' Sounds like a story I used to read when I was a boy."

Something about my manner must have told him how much in earnest I was, for he stopped laughing all at once and began to talk seriously to me.

"Well, let's see," he said, turning toward his desk. "Here is a chart with a schedule of the faculty. Have you thought what you might substitute for drawing if you were permitted to drop it?"

"Yes," I said promptly. "French."

"French? You, a freshman? It's over a month late now and we could hardly ask Monsieur de Bussiers—"

"I've already asked him, and he says it's all right with him. He says his beginning class has had nothing but verbs so far, and he'll help me make up that work after school. I'll take all the French that's offered at South High, if you'll only let me drop freehand drawing."

"At least you don't exactly seem to be trying to get out of work," Mr. Ozias said, smiling.

I liked French so much that I took two years of it, and I became so interested in the study of languages that I also took three years each of German and Latin before I finished high school.

Years later, when I was a teacher myself, I realized more than I did at the time how kind Monsieur de Bussiers was to take on that extra work with me after he had had a full day of teaching, and I never ceased to be grateful to him for it.

The freshman assembly room was extremely dark, and I was always afraid that I would walk down the wrong aisle when I entered the room from the front, as I had to, and that I wouldn't be able to find my own seat. I was nervous, too, before so many students, for fear I might do something wrong and so appear ridiculous to them.

On the last day of the first semester, I was unusually late in returning to assembly because I had stopped asking my algebra teacher about something I didn't understand. When I walked across the wide space in front of the room, it seemed to me that I was the only freshman who wasn't in his seat. I dashed over to my aisle and was halfway down it and not far from my own seat in the back of the room when there was a capping of hands and laughing throughout the room. I felt my checks go hot and I tugged at my tic and collar and belt to make sure that they were in place, and I glanced down to see whether my petticoat showed. Since I could find

nothing wrong I joined the laughing and cheering, pretending to be a good sport about whatever was taking place.

All the rest of the day I worried over what had happened in the assembly hall. At last, when Winnie, the girl who sat across the aisle from me, and I were getting ready to go home and were alone in the cloakroom together, I picked up courage enough to ask her what had caused the commotion among the students that morning.

"Why, Borghild, I thought you knew," she exclaimed in surprise. "Your name, with Charles Hixon's and Adelaide Swinburne's, was on the board for having the highest honor ratings in the freshman class this semester."

It was silly of me to be so sensitive about the children at South High School. All the four years I was there they treated me with the utmost kindness and consideration. They were a good-natured, democratic crowd, always willing to give anyone a fair chance. I became great friends with many of them and I enjoyed myself so thoroughly that I brought home unsatisfactory marks in deportment for whispering too much during school hours.

I had difficulty following the demonstrations of geometry theorems on the board unless I was perfectly prepared, and then I sometimes wasn't sure I had things right. However, with the exception of a few points which my father cleared up for me, I managed to get along pretty well in the class.

Once, because I hadn't been able to see what was going on, I won praise, which embarrassed me very much.

It was about parallel angles, and the problem I was trying to solve depended upon something I had missed in class the preceding day. My father was out of town, so I struggled along by myself for hours. At last, I thought I had found a solution that worked out satisfactorily.

The following day I was called upon to demonstrate the original theorem. I was nervous as I stood at the board, for I was pretty sure that I was not using the right method.

When I had finished, Miss Swain, my teacher, exclaimed, "Why, Borghild, that is ingenious. It shows original thinking. I wish more of you in the class would take the trouble to explore beyond your texts."

After that incident, my opinion was frequently asked about original theorems. It was a good thing it was near the end of the term, for it wouldn't have taken long for someone to discover that I knew much less about geometry than the class suspected.

When I was a senior I came under the influence of Miss Evelyn Watts, who was the senior room principal and also my teacher in literature. There were more than a hundred of us students in the senior room, and as our literature class was large, too, no one

became intimately acquainted with Miss Watts. She wasn't the kind of person students became intimately acquainted with anyway. But she made us all feel that whatever we did counted for a great deal with her, and she had an uncanny way of telling us our weakest and our strongest points.

In literature class she presented fiction characters so vividly that I never forgot them. After she had finished lecturing on an author, I felt I knew exactly what sort of human being he was and what he had tried to put across in his books.

We had been studying Addison and Steele and when we had finished reading about them and had listened to Miss Watts lecture, she told us to write a theme that would have some bearing on the work we had covered. I wrote a Sir Roger de Coverley paper, imitating the style of the authors and putting Sir Roger in a modern roller-skating rink.

"You have done the job of imitating Addison and Steele very well," Miss Watts told me. "I think someday you will be able to write creditably in your own style." I must have looked doubtful, for she said, "I really mean it."

This praise from Miss Watts pleased me, for she was never wasteful of her compliments. I secretly wished I could write well someday, but it seemed something too far beyond me to really hope for. In the seventh grade I had had a story accepted by the Journal Junior, a supplement of the Minneapolis Journal, which was devoted entirely to the stories of children who were interested in writing. In high school I contributed regularly to the Journal Junior and won several prizes. I was appointed by the editor of this paper, Miss Mae Harris Anson, to be the reporter for South High. But, after all, none of this could be counted as any real literary achievement.

The praise from Miss Watts was an incentive for me to try much harder with my writing. I was rewarded by being chosen as the class poet, and when our senior annual was published my class poem appeared in it.

I tried out for debating and entered several oratorical contests, but I didn't place in any of them. After the last tryout in my senior year, I felt pretty much discouraged. Miss Watts called me to her desk the following afternoon.

"I have been watching you today," she said. "You are beginning to feel as though you have failed in public speaking because you were not chosen to be one of the winners. Whether you placed or not, in these contests you have entered, may have been merely a matter of opinion of the judges, you know. If you keep trying, you are going to meet a judge someday who likes what you say. Then you will be ready for the real victory because you will have learned to appreciate what it costs."

At the end of my senior year, I was asked to be one of the speakers at the commencement exercises.

The day following my graduation from high school I met one of our neighbors on the street.

"You were beautiful last night," she told me. "You had one of the prettiest dresses of all the graduates; and your oration was fine, too. But I was telling my husband how too bad it was that you read your program during the exercises, so you showed everyone how nearsighted you were. The lights were reflected in your glasses, and nobody would have noticed your eyes if it hadn't been for that."

The reminder cut me to the quick, but I knew what she said was true. In my eagerness to see my name on the printed program I forgot to practice my usual caution of waiting until I came home to look at anything that was given me in public.

I didn't answer, but I told myself that, if I could help it, no one was going to have a chance to make such a remark about me again.

Strangely enough it was physical training that worried me most during my freshman year at the university. I had mathematics class immediately following physical training and the two were a block apart. I always had to rush to get into my clothes and go from the Armory over to Folwell Hall; and if we were kept on the floor in physical training for even a minute after the bell rang, I became madly excited. I imagined that in my haste some of my clothes would go on wrong and I would make a sight of myself, especially standing in front of the mathematics class while explaining a problem on the board. With the other girls, dressing was a simple matter. One glance in the mirror told them whether everything about their appearance was as it should be. I, however, was in the habit of going over my clothes carefully, feeling every part of them, and this made my dressing very slow. I wore twenty-three separate articles in those days, for I counted them once, and my clothes were typical of the average college girl's school outfit. Just keeping track of all this paraphernalia in my locker was a chore.

At our Christmas party we were dressed in elaborate costumes instead of our regular gym suits, and after it was over, I carried half my clothes in my schoolbag to my mathematics class.

"You may put the first problem for today on the board," Professor Shumway told me as soon as I barged into his classroom.

"I'm not prepared," I said.

"Try it," he encouraged me.

"I just can't," I told him.

He looked at me in disgust.

"We are far enough along now so you should be able to work this problem without any preparation," he said.

I couldn't very well tell him that I had neither a collar nor a tie on and that I was holding my belt, which had slipped off, in my hand. Later, when we began to use the running track in physical training, I had a still harder time with it. The running track extended along the balcony high above the main floor and was poorly lit. After several narrow escapes when I almost pitched headlong down into the main part of the gymnasium, I knew I should have to do something if I was to continue with the others. So early one morning I went to the Armory before anyone else was there and walked slowly around the track. I examined every pan. of it carefully, and I crawled on my hands and knees in the darkest places to make sure I wasn't missing anything over which I could stumble. When I had satisfied myself that I was entirely familiar with the track, I went for a trial spin. After that I didn't have any more accidents and I was no longer afraid.

During the second semester of my freshman year, I began to have trouble with trigonometry, which all of us had to take. I couldn't follow the board work because I couldn't see the figures. The reading of the logarithm tables, which were printed in very small figures in our text, was difficult for me, too. Toward the end of the term, I found myself in a group that was dangerously near to failing.

"I'd be ashamed to have to admit that a daughter of mine failed in mathematics," my father said when I told him of my predicament. "What seems to be the trouble?"

I never liked to admit to my father that I couldn't see things, but this time there was no escaping it.

"Why didn't you tell me before?" he asked. "I'm sure I can help you."

For weeks after that we worked together in the evenings. He read columns of logarithm tables aloud to me and coached me on essential formulas and helped me with typical problems.

At the end of the semester, I passed trigonometry with a grade of Good.

"You had a much better grasp of the subject than I gave you credit for," Professor Shumway told me when I met him later. "You answered everything basic in the examination questions."

At the end of the first semester of my sophomore year, just when examinations were about to begin, my father died very suddenly from heart failure. It was my first great grief, and the world was a changed place for me after his death. I missed his jolly companionship and his keen interest in everything I did.

He had bought his favorite music pieces and sat for hours with me listening to make sure that I played them right. While we were at the lake during the summer, he rowed over to the station every Sunday for a paper so I could know whether my story had been printed in the Journal Junior that week. He drew beautiful maps for me to help me in geography and history. And he always urged me to do my best in my regular classwork at school.

"Can't you do just a little better?" he would ask.

Once, out of sheer habit, he asked me that question when I brought home my report card from high school.

"But I got ninety-eight in two of my subjects," I told him, hurt that he had not appreciated my efforts any more than

After he was gone things were harder at home, too. My mother grieved and worried, and from the first she depended upon me to help her with her business affairs and the housework (we rented out several rooms in our house right away) and with the care of the younger children. I realized that I should have to earn my own living as soon as possible and I decided that I would become an English teacher. I could stay at home until I had received my bachelor's degree from the university. I gave up the pipe organ lessons which my father had recently arranged for me to take and, instead, I secured as many piano pupils as I could to help pay for my books and tuition at school.

I kept postponing my science class because I couldn't make up my mind what to take. I had tried physics in high school; but because of precise work in the laboratory, I had had to drop it. Since physics had been an elective, that had not worried me; for I had plenty of language credits which I could substitute for it. But at college a minor was required in science.

I studied the catalogue and tried to figure out what I could take. At last, I thought I had hit upon the very thing. There was a four-semester course in geology which made no mention of laboratory work.

The first year of geology went beautifully. The textbooks and the lectures of the professors covered everything I had to know, and all I did was to take notes carefully on both and commit them to memory. The field trips for the geology and geography of Minnesota were fun, and I had begun to heave a sigh of relief because I had almost finished my science minor when all of a sudden I found myself in such deep water that I thought at first I wasn't going to be able to graduate from the College of Science, Literature, and the Arts of the university.

For the last semester's work in science I registered for something that looked just as good to me in the catalogue as the other courses had, and I started out just as confidently. However, after the first few days I began to have misgivings; for when the professor held up rocks to the class and asked their chemical compounds, everyone but me seemed to be able to answer him correctly. I couldn't understand where the rest of the students had secured their information, and after I had failed for the fourth or fifth time, I asked the young man sitting next to me how he and everyone else could recognize the contents of the rocks at sight.

"That's easy," he said. "We got that in chemistry." "Has everyone in the class had chemistry?" I asked.

"Sure," he answered. "It's a prerequisite of the course."

I gasped.

"Do you mean to say that you haven't had chemistry?" he asked.

I just kept staring at him.

He shrugged his shoulders.

"You're going to have one swell time in here without it." "But I simply have to have this credit for my science minor," I told him. "What in the world am I going to do? Isn't there any way I can learn the chemical compounds of the rocks and get the hang of the rest well enough to pass the course?"

He thought for a minute.

"I have a book at home that might help you," he said, "but I doubt that you will be able to remember half the stuff without having had the work in class."

"I could try," I said.

The young man brought the book and for weeks I committed to memory endless lists of formulas that meant absolutely nothing to me. At the end of the semester, I felt as though I had earned three credits in mental gymnastics rather than in paleontology, under which name the course was listed in the catalogue.

I continued with my study of German and French at the university, and I also accepted Old and Middle English, which were almost like two other foreign languages.

"Why do you study so many languages and yet never think any more about the one that belongs to your own people?" my mother asked me one day when she heard me reciting a selection from Caedmon's Song of the Creation.

"I haven't studied nearly all of them yet," I told her airily. "There's Spanish and Italian and—"

"You know what I mean," she interrupted. "I had you read Norwegian before you started public school and you were confirmed in it. It would be easy for you to take it up again."

"But why, Mother?"

"Norway has a beautiful literature and it would not hurt you at all to read some of it in the original. I used to think you liked Norwegian when you were a little girl," she finished wistfully.

So, to please my mother I chose Norwegian as one of my senior electives. But I dreaded the drudgery of another be-ginning course in a foreign language and I decided that I would skip it in Norwegian if I could manage it.

I went to Professor Bothne, who was at the head of the Norwegian department, and told him I was of Norwegian descent and would like to study the Norwegian classics, but that I didn't want to waste my time on elementary courses. He handed me a little brown book that lay on his desk.

"Read this grammar and come back in a week," he said. "We'll give you an examination then and see whether you know as much about Norwegian as you think you do."

I was very embarrassed. I hadn't intended to impress him with my knowledge of Norwegian. But I was in for it now, and there was nothing to do but to go through with it.

I returned in a week as he told me.

"The only thing I noticed that was peculiar to Norwegian grammar," I said as I sat waiting for the examination to begin, "was that the definite article becomes a suffix to the noun without modifiers."

The remark seemed to please him. After a few simple questions he closed his book*

"I guess you'll do," he said, looking at me smiling. "Report in my literature class tomorrow."

That was for me the beginning of a pleasant excursion into Norwegian literature. I read Ibsen, Bjornson, Jonas Lie, Wergeland, Wellhaven, Vinje, and many other old masters, and the modern ones as well. I found that I was doing much more than pleasing my mother by studying Norwegian literature at college.

But with all my best efforts it is doubtful that I should have been able to carry on at the university if it had not been for the kindness of my friends there. My two most intimate ones, Nellie Wheelock, and Laura Oberg were always looking out for me. They found seats for me in crowded classrooms, helped me down dark and unfamiliar stairways, let me borrow their notes which they had copied from blackboards I couldn't see, located places and people for me on die campus, and did a thousand other favors for me that saved me both time and trouble.

Often, they left notes in my post office box.

"Borghild, did you know there is a poster in Folwell Hall saying that our English class won't meet today?"

"I'm buying the new history text that Professor White recommended yesterday. Why don't you plan to meet me on the steps in front of the library and we'll go over to the bookstore together? Didn't you say you wanted to pick up some other things over there, too?"

"Woodrow Wilson, the Governor of New Jersey, is speaking in chapel today. Hurry over as quickly as you can. I'll be looking for you at the west door."

Nellie Wheelock was in many of my English and history classes. There was a great deal of outside reading required in both of these subjects, and she used to read aloud to me by the hour. This saved my eye, and it also fixed the material she covered so firmly in my mind that I seldom had to review it for examinations.

Both Nellie Wheelock and Laura belonged to the little group of girls called Sigma Betas that I had been going around with since I was a freshman. At first a few of us from South High—Laura Oberg, Anna Hanson, Myrtle Turnquist, Ebba Norman, and I—got into the habit of eating our noon lunches we brought from home together in the small dining room at Shevlin Hall. Soon we became acquainted with a bunch from Central who sat at a table near ours. Then a few girls from out of town joined us. After a little we were going on hikes together and having little parties, and then we organized into a regular society and called ourselves Sigma Betas. We were an entirely social organization, but to me the little group meant much more than that. It raised my morale to be included among such attractive and interesting girls and, since they were very much alert to everything that went on around the campus, just from being with them I learned many things it was good to know.

The spring we were seniors, everyone who expected to teach was excited about positions. The girls compared and exchanged application pictures, checked one another's majors and minors to see what they should say, in their applications, they could teach, and talked about the recommendations they received from their professors.

I listened to all this talk without joining in any of it. I needed to earn my living more than any of the other girls, for the burden of keeping our large household having Esther and me at the university was becoming too much for my mother. She worried constantly about money, and it seemed to me that she grieved more and more for my father. But whenever I thought of teaching, I wondered whether my eyes were going to make things hard for me, as they had done in everything else, I had tried.

Without discussing my plans with anyone, therefore, I set about to do what I could toward securing a position for the coming year. I was all right as far as teaching subjects were concerned. I had German, French, Norwegian, English, and history. Theoretically I could teach geology, but I wouldn't take any chances of running into unnecessary difficulties by mentioning that. I had my application pictures taken and I was overjoyed to find that in the slight profile that the photographer had taken of me my bad eye didn't show at all. I practiced writing application letters until I could do this satisfactorily. Then I went to one of my professors and asked him for a recommendation to teach.

"Why do you want to teach?" he asked me.

"I have to make my living," I told him, "and, besides, I've been preparing to do that all through college."

"With your eyes?" he asked.

"I've had them all my life," I told him, my heart beginning to thump, "and they haven't prevented me from getting through school. I'm going to graduate this spring."

"That's entirely different," he said.

'Why is it different?" I asked.

He looked straight at me.

"I may as well be frank with you," he said. "I doubt very much that any school board or superintendent could be persuaded to hire you. And even though you did secure a position it is my opinion that you would not be able to hold it. Students nowadays simply wouldn't put up with a teacher with such eyes. They would laugh at you and ridicule you; and you would find it difficult, I am afraid, to gain the confidence of the parents, too, for they would not believe that you could see well enough to do the work."

"But," I faltered, "what would you suggest that I should do?"

He thought for a minute.

"I really can't say. You will have to work out that problem for yourself. After all, you know your own situation best. I am sorry to have to say this to you, because your work in class has been very satisfactory; but I simply can't encourage you to teach. I am reasonably sure that you wouldn't survive one semester."

For days after this conversation with my professor I went around so utterly miserable that I thought I couldn't go on living. I felt apologetic about being on the campus at all. I avoided speaking to the students I knew, even though I recognized them. I tried to hide my face so my professors wouldn't have to look at me.

Finally, one afternoon I gave up the struggle altogether. Instead of going to literature class I took the path that led down to the riverbank.

"What's the use of trying anyway?" I asked myself bitterly.

I sat down on a green knoll that jutted out into the water, and I watched the swift current of the Mississippi as it swept past me. The river was high, and it washed up against the bluffs on the opposite side from which I was sitting. Pretty soon my attention

was attracted by some whirling eddies that stopped the steady flow of the water, but farther downstream the current swept on as though nothing had been in its way.

Why, that was the way it was with me, I told myself. Things were forever getting in my way, but they couldn't stop me. Not unless I let them as I was beginning to do now.

I dried my tears and got to my feet. After one deep breath of the fresh air that blew in from the river I started back toward the campus.

Before I entered my classroom in literature, where I would have to face the students, who would wonder why I came in so near the end of the period, I held the doorknob for a second.

"I'll be a high school English teacher," I said under my breath. "I tell you, I will. And a good one, too."

The next day I picked up courage enough to go to Miss Whitney, my rhetoric professor, and tell her about my experience when I had tried to get a recommendation to teach.

"Do you really want to teach?" Miss Whitney asked a little brusquely.

"Yes, I do," I answered.

"More than anything else?"

"More than anything else I know how to do now."

She looked hard at me for a minute.

"Then," she said gently, "go ahead and do it. One of the best teachers I ever knew conducted her classes while she lay in a plaster cast. And I can't remember that her students threw a single brick at her."

I was too grateful to speak.

"I'll send in your recommendations today," she went on.

I rose and tried to thank her.

"I am only too glad to do it," she said, "and I hope you will get along as well as I think you will,"

I turned to leave.

"Wait," she said. "I'd like to have you go to see Maria Sanford. She hasn't had you in class, but she knows of you and is interested in you."

I must have shown my surprise. Maria Stanford was perhaps the most outstanding and the best-beloved professor on the university campus. It seemed unbelievable that she would even know of my existence, since I had had no occasion to go to her before.

"I have told her about you," Miss Whitney explained.

As I went down the corridor on the third floor in Folwell Hall, I felt as though I were walking on air. Miss Whitney was supposed to be one of the unapproachables on the faculty and she had spoken to the great Maria Sanford about me and got her interested in me.

I found Maria Sanford sitting at her desk. Her snowy hair was parted in the middle and combed straight back and, as usual, she was wearing a plain black dress relieved only by a white niching at the top of her high collar, and a long gold watch chain. She listened attentively without interrupting me until I had finished what I had to say. Then she left her chair and came over to me and put her hand in mine.

"I wouldn't let my eyes worry me too much if I were you," she said in that deep, musical voice of hers, "for in spite of them you have already accomplished more than most young people your age. We all have handicaps, you know. Mental, moral, spiritual. Yours is only physical."

Chapter 3

One morning while I was helping my mother wash clothes before starting off for my first class at the university, the doorbell rang.

"I'll answer it," my mother told me. "I have to go upstairs anyway to make the starch."

Pretty soon I heard her calling me.

"Come up quick," she said excitedly.

I rushed upstairs, wiping my hands on my apron as I ran.

"There's a letter for you from the clerk of the school board at Twin Valley," she said, handing me a long white envelope.

My hands trembled so I could scarcely open it. But after reading the letter inside I thought I must be mistaken in what it said.

"You read it," I said, handing my mother the letter.

After a little she said, "He's sending you a teacher's contract. You are to be the assistant principal of the school."

Together we examined the legal-looking document that accompanied the letter.

"It's for nine months and you are to have sixty dollars a month," my mother exclaimed.

Her voice broke and she sat down in the rocker near the bay window of the sitting room, where we had been standing.

"Thank God, my prayers have been answered," she said, folding her hands.

A few days later another contract arrived for me. This one was from the school board at Sacred Hearts Minnesota.

"You had better sign the one from Twin Valley," my mother told me. "Enoch and Elizabeth are there and they have invited you to stay with them, you know. For the first year, at least, I would feel better about you if you were up there."

I took my mother's advice and accepted the position at Twin Valley.

After that I told the girls at the university of my good fortune. I could discuss teaching positions with them and join them in the fun they were having—imagining encounters with irate parents, eccentric superintendents, and slow school boards—now that I was the first one among them to have a job for the coming year.

"The lady with the multiple teaching contracts," they called me.

Laura Oberg and I marched together in the academic procession at the baccalaureate services and on commencement day. I was not able to follow the address of the commencement speaker, for I was so happy.

'Well, Borghild Dahl," I told myself as I sat beside Laura, "eyes or no eyes, you have succeeded in getting this far, anyway."

The summer following my graduation I was so busy that I didn't worry as much as I otherwise might have done. Esther and I worked in Minneapolis while the rest of the family were at the lake. With the money we earned we bought material which my mother made up into beautiful clothes for both of us.

"Maybe, if I am dressed attractively, they won't mind me so much," I told myself when I saw the lovely things my mother was finishing for me: tan wool voile trimmed with pale blue panne velvet, a dark blue serge sailor suit with red braid on the collar and cuffs, a dark blue suit with several pretty blouses to wear with it, and a blue plaid French gingham which was to be for my first day of teaching.

However, the words of the professor who had not been able to recommend me for a teaching position kept coming back to me.

"Students nowadays simply wouldn't put up with a teacher with such eyes."

I made the train trip alone from Minneapolis to Twin Valley. It took about six hours, and before I reached there, I had worked myself up into a frenzy. Suppose I became the laughingstock of the school. It would be terribly embarrassing for Uncle Enoch and Aunt Elizabeth to have such a niece living with them. Why hadn't I thought of that earlier and gone where no one knew me, so I would be the only one to suffer if the worst should happen?

The wholehearted welcome which Uncle Enoch and Aunt Elizabeth gave me when I stepped off the train made me forget my worries for a while. But when I was in bed that night, I felt worse than ever, like a thief who had stolen into a place where he had no business to be.

Aunt Elizabeth went out on the porch with me the next morning when I started off for school.

"I know you are going to get along beautifully," she said. "You always do, you know."

A mower was cutting the tall weeds on the school grounds and the air was strong with their sharp tang. Inside the schoolhouse I was greeted by the familiar smell of sweeping compound and chalk dust.

I went directly to the superintendent's office on the second floor.
"Doc told me you had come," he said, shaking my hand cordially, "and I was expecting you."

As he talked to me, there was not the slightest hint that he found anything unusual about my appearance. He treated me exactly as he might have done with any other girl who had come to teach under him.

"We are trying to offer four years of high school for the first time in our history," he went on to say. "I am hoping to prevail upon three of our young people who were juniors last year to stay here and finish their course. Raymond Hansom is a prince of a fellow, and the two girls, Anna Holm and Mabel Sethney, are excellent students."

He and I would teach all the subjects in the high school, he went on to say, and I would also take charge of the class in United States history in the eighth grade.

"We will not be accredited," he said, "and so our students will receive their high school credits only by passing the state examinations. And their work will have to be of a high enough standard so they will be prepared to pass entrance examinations in higher institutions, should they decide to go there."

The superintendent and I then went into the high school assembly room, where on the board he made a list of the subjects we were to teach. He would take mathematics and sciences, he said, and English and history and the languages would be left to me.

Several students came into the high school assembly before we finished our discussion.

"We might as well begin right now to work out tentative programs for those who are here," the superintendent said. "We'll have to be careful about the credits for the seniors so they will be ready to graduate in the spring. And the juniors will bear watching, too. We can be more elastic about the freshmen and sophomores because they will have plenty of time to get in the subjects they need."

By noon, the superintendent and I had succeeded in making only a temporary schedule for ourselves. I would combine freshman and sophomore English in one class, and junior and senior English in another. United States history in the eighth grade would be my third subject, and some high school history my fourth. German and Norwegian were both to be offered. There might have to be two classes in German to take care of those just beginning and those who had already had one year of it, but there would be only one class in Norwegian. Several students asked for Latin and a large number wanted bookkeeping. The latter was especially popular among the older students who came to school after they had heard there was to be a full four-year high school course offered. Since the superintendent's time was already all taken up, I would have to teach both of these last subjects.

"Will our children really be high school graduates after they have finished the school here?" one mother asked me that afternoon.

"Yes," I answered, "providing they pass the state examinations, and we are going to do all we can to help them do that."

"I never expected to be able to afford a high school education for all my children," a farmer in blue overalls said to me. "But when they can come home every night and help with the chores and I won't have to pay out cash for their board and room, I think I can make it."

In the late afternoon when the last student was gone, I was exhausted. I looked around the little high school assembly room. The sun was still pouring through the crisp white curtains of the west windows, casting its reflection in the glass covering the face of the clock and tinting the green wall around it with a warm gold. There were scraps of paper left on the rows of worn desks in front of me; and the large globe on the gilt pedestal and the rolls of maps were piled in the corner at my left, where they had been shoved so the students could see the writing the superintendent and I had put on the blackboard.

Then I remembered the laughter and the ridicule that I was supposed to have aroused among the students. I had been so busy all day that I had forgotten to give it a thought until now. I could still see those earnest parents with whom I had been talking—most of them Scandinavian pioneers in the Red River Valley—and their children, scarcely less eager for the education we were trying to offer them. And I knew that if I was to be a laughingstock among them those who were to make me one had not yet put in their appearance.

Even though I had a model group to work with, I realized from the first that the less conscious I made them of my eyes the better it would be for me. I couldn't very well change the appearance of my eyes, but I could, at least to a certain extent, conceal from my high school students how very little I could see with them. I still remembered what the neighbor woman had said to me the day after I graduated from high school.

It was most important to be careful in my eighth-grade history class, I knew at once. There were almost forty children in it, and since they were younger, they would be more likely to be up to mischief than those in the high school. At college I had committed to memory in chronological order the names of the Presidents of the United States and the dates of their administrations. With these in mind it was easy to fit in detailed events which had occurred while the Presidents were in office. The chapters in the text made convenient assignments and so I didn't have to worry about seeing to read while I conducted this class.

In teaching English history and English literature, I found that I had a similar advantage, for I had committed to memory the dates of the Kings of England from Alfred the Great to George V. Since I had had extensive work in English history and English literature, I needed only to brush up on these two subjects to be able to present them to my students. However, I had to familiarize myself thoroughly with the texts they used in order to know what was included in them, especially when I pretended to be reading from the books in assigning the work for the following day.

I learned to take short cuts in organizing material in American literature. For instance, in placing groups of writers in my mind I tried to think of something they had in common. I took the date 1809, which seemed to be just about the time when most of the authors about whom I had to teach were born. Then I added to this the normal span of life—threescore years and ten—making 1879 the year they normally should have died. After I had tabulated the main exceptions and tried to remember why they failed to reach that age, I also made a note of those who had lived much longer.

Since I knew the main events that had taken place in American history during those years, it was a simple matter to weave them into the events in the authors' lives. Take Longfellow, for instance. His friendships could be largely accounted for in this way, and even the dates for the publication of his works and what he wrote. He lived during the time of the great Concord men of letters, and his home at Cambridge was not far from Concord; so, it was natural he should have associated with these authors.

Remembering this, I made a list of the authors who actually did live in Concord.

I found that recalling little gossipy stories about writers and places of interest helped to keep them in my mind; and the children enjoyed the stories, too. Thoreau's demanding from Emerson why he hadn't come to jail with him instead of paying the poll tax, and Whittier's dashes for liberty away from prying females who intruded on the privacy of his bachelor home, and Longfellow's bright vests and escapades while he was a gay widower—all were incidents which the students liked to hear and remembered.

If there were long lists of things I needed to know, I arranged them in alphabetical order first and then learned them. If there were events in history, I placed them in chronological order. Repeating things over and over while I walked to school, or dressed or did anything else mechanical, helped to fix facts in my mind.

I took outstanding cities in the world and tried to remember important people in history and literature who had lived in them. London, Edinburgh, Paris, New York, and Philadelphia proved to be real gold mines of information for me. I also listed rivers, lakes, mountains, and forests and associated them with events and people. It was surprising how these devices, which would probably seem senseless to other people, helped me to train my memory and finally to organize for ready use the masses of material that I was gradually accumulating.

The teaching of languages demanded much more intense study than that required for my preparation in history and literature. The translations of my students in class had to be accurate and in good diction. This meant that in order to teach without seeing what was in the book I had to very nearly memorize every classic that was studied. I used to start out by reading each part of the classic for the first time about a week before I presented it in class. By going over it every day I knew it by heart when the time came for the students to translate it for me. When the students had finished studying Storm's Immensee, Chamisso's Peter Schlemihl, and Bjornson's A Happy Boy, I felt as familiar with them as though I had written them myself.

It was important for me that I should learn to know my students as early as possible and that I should be able to recognize them afterward without having to go right up close to them. I had to do a lot of thinking and planning to bring this about.

Although the voices of very young people are generally not so characteristic of them as are those of mature people, I knew I should have to depend upon voices a great deal in distinguishing my students. At the end of the first day, I knew many of their voices. At the end of the week, I knew all of them.

After I had seated my students alphabetically in the assembly room and in my classes, I began to commit to memory their names from my record book. For each day I set myself the task of being able to pick out a certain number of my pupils. I first repeated their surnames to myself and then the combination of these with their Christian names. For example, in the first row in my senior English class there might have been five seats. According to my chart these belonged to Froshaug, Hanson, Holm, Sethney, and Solien. After these were firmly fixed in my mind, I told myself the seats belonged to Esther Froshaug, Raymond Hanson, Anna Holm, Mabel Sethney, and Clara Solien. If there were several students whose surnames were the same, or if they had the same initial, it was easier to learn the class roll. The same was true if there were many by the same Christian name.

After this I looked carefully at the students to see whether there wasn't something about them that might help me to recognize them when they were not in their seats. I tried to remember their clothes. This was not hard in those days in Twin Valley because most of the children had only one or two outfits for school all year. Besides, many of their mothers made their clothes at home and so there was much more individuality in their dressing than there would have been had their clothes been bought ready-made.

I learned to associate the students with the kinds of papers they handed in to me, too. I had plenty of opportunity to do this because my teaching of English and beginning languages meant endless stacks of them. Uncle Enoch and Aunt Elizabeth thought I was too conscientious about my papers, but I knew that, aside from the good it was doing the students to have their mistakes pointed out to them, I was being more than repaid for my work by the knowledge about my pupils that I was gaining from it.

There were many things about these papers that gave me valuable information: the general appearance, the handwriting, and the content. After going over piles of papers I identified odors from them with the whiffs I got when certain students were near me. For instance, one paper reeked of cheap tobacco and pretty soon I found a chubby boy in the freshman class whose clothes were saturated with the same smell. There was one girl who must have spent all her pocket money on spicy perfume, for she sprinkled it over every paper she handed in and on everything she wore. Several of the boys from the country worked in the barns at home and I could usually detect a slight odor from their clothes and sometimes from their papers, although this was not always the case. Several students must have come from homes which were not thoroughly aired, for their papers and clothes had a stale smell suggestive of cooked foods. A boy in the front seat in the assembly room chewed cloves continually, another must have lived on onions, and a girl always smelled of Ivory soap.

Whenever I heard something about any particular student, I tried to remember it, because it helped me to place that child in my mind. One boy who was often late for school helped to support his widowed mother and his siblings. Another worked at the hardware store evenings and Saturdays, and so he seldom had any time for study outside of school. The sister of one girl in several of my classes had just been jilted on the eve of her marriage to what was supposed to have been a model young man in the community. The father of one of my boys was the town miser, and two sisters in high school lived in the finest home in Twin Valley. One girl, it was whispered, wasn't quite nice; another had been going with a man much older than herself and she would probably marry him as soon as she had finished high school, if not before.

I didn't try to find out these things, but they came to me without my asking because the town was small, and everyone knew everything about everyone else.

The Friday afternoon that the superintendent handed me my salary check for the month of September, I felt that I was the richest and the happiest person in the world. There had been no hint from anyone, either, that this was to be my last salary check or that I hadn't earned it. The job was still mine. I was making good.

I rushed down to the bank to cash my check.

"Will you have it put into savings or in a checking account?" the clerk asked me.

I looked at him blankly. I had had visions of his handing me sixty silver dollars from behind the wicket window.

"Oh, a—a checking account," I stammered.

"Not any of it in savings?" he inquired.

"No," I told him. "No, I'm not ready for that yet."

He wrote something in a small book, placed a sheaf of narrow yellow slips of paper in a leather case, and handed it to me.

I hurried home to show Uncle Enoch and Aunt Elizabeth my new bank account. It was the first one I had ever had.

"Fifty dollars of it are yours," Uncle Enoch told me. "Your mother charged me only ten dollars a month while I was at the university, and Mother and I won't take any more from you."

Sixty dollars a month. I had worked and saved all year for the twenty I had paid for my tuition at the university.

Five dollars would easily buy all the postage I needed, and a hundred other things. I could send my mother forty-five dollars every month and she would never have to worry about money again.

Before Christmas I hurried up to the last minute at school. Examinations and reports for the fourth month had to be gotten out of the way before the holidays, and we put on the last of a series of benefit programs for a much-needed piano. This program netted us enough so I could select the piano in Minneapolis when I went down there.

On the last day before vacation the children of the entire school gathered in the high school assembly room to sing Christmas carols. The janitor acted as Santa Claus and brought candy and popcorn for everyone. We teachers also received gifts from our pupils. Mine was a souvenir spoon with the picture of the school building engraved in the bowl of it and the name Twin Valley, Minnesota, on the handle.

While I was on the train that day, I was so happy I thought I should burst. Here was I, going home for a vacation like any other high school teacher, my bags full of gifts I had received from Uncle Enoch's family, the teachers, and students I worked with, and other friends I had made in Twin Valley. And I had presents for everyone at home.

The house in Minneapolis, which I had always taken for granted, looked cozier and lovelier than I had remembered it. My mother had cleaned and polished it until it shone, and the piano had been refinished for my home coming. My mother had also baked and cooked all sorts of good things, and it seemed to me that there was some sort of surprise every time I turned around.

The days flew by, and before I knew it the last one of my vacations had arrived.

"With all the fun I've had at home," I told my mother, "I don't mind going back to work one bit. We have lots of fun at Twin Valley, too."

I had my bags packed and was just going up to bed a little early, so that I would be ready to take the train in the morning, when my mother called me.

"Come into the sitting room," she said. "I have something to say to you."

She closed the door so we wouldn't disturb the rest of the family upstairs. At the grave expression on her face, I became alarmed at once, and she, seeing this, smiled at me.

"Oh, it's nothing you need to worry about," she told me. "I almost decided not to mention it. But you will be gone for so long now—it is almost three months before Easter—that I thought it would be best to do it, anyway."

"But, Mother, what is it?" I asked.

"Now, now, don't get excited. As I said, it is nothing to be alarmed about. It is only that I haven't seemed to be able to shake off the aftereffects of that cold I caught last fall. Even after that visit with Olga when I had a good rest, it hung on and I couldn't get back to where I was before."

My mother had never been ill that I could remember, and I became thoroughly frightened. I said she should have told me about how badly she felt as soon as I came home.

"I didn't have the heart to do that," she said, her voice soft with tears. "You were so happy."

I insisted that I would stay over in Minneapolis for a few days and take her to a doctor.

"Don't be foolish," she said, trying to act brusque. "You know very well that the best thing you can do for me is to go back to your teaching. It has been wonderful not to have to worry about money this year."

She promised she would go to a doctor by herself the next day and wrote to me telling me exactly what he said to her.

As soon as I returned to Twin Valley, I told Uncle Enoch about my mother. He looked grave and asked me a few questions, but he said very little except that no one could diagnose a case without seeing the patient. A few days later he suddenly decided to go

down to Minneapolis to see my mother. After his return I learned that an exploratory operation had been performed on her and that the surgeon had found she was in the last stages of cancer. A weaker person would have been dead long before this. With her vitality my mother would probably live five or six months more.

That bleak day in January, when Uncle Enoch told me this, was the zero hour of my life.

After we could talk more calmly, we decided that it would be best for me to continue to teach during the months of February and March. Ellen and a cousin of my mother's, Bertha Swan, would care for my mother until the first of April, when Bertha would have to leave. The financial assistance I could give during those months would help a great deal.

When it was time for me to leave for Minneapolis, Aunt Elizabeth came with me. She brought the baby along with her so my mother could see him.

After Aunt Elizabeth had gone back to Twin Valley, we children were left alone with my mother. I spent hours reading aloud to her, at first stories and novels and later only passages from the Bible. She liked St. John the best. It seemed to me that the beautiful words from this gospel were my mother's instead of Christ's.

Toward the end my mother could not lie down in bed. She sat in the Morris chair beside the fireplace, for the spring was late and we kept a fire burning on the grate all the time.

One of the last nights she lived, when everyone else was asleep, she began to talk to me.

"We have both known for a long time how this must end," she said softly. "But it hasn't been easy for either of us to talk about it, has it?"

She stopped as if she expected me to answer her, but I couldn't speak. A sudden flame from the fire lit the room and I could see her clearly. Her eyes were fixed tenderly upon me.

"You and I have understood each other so well," she went on to say. "Perhaps because we have needed each other so much. You have been a great joy to me and have made me very happy. Sometimes it may be a comfort to you to remember how much I have loved you and what I am going to say to you tonight.

"I used to worry about your eyes. But long ago I stopped being that foolish. I know that, whatever happens, God will watch over you and guide you. It was only at first, when your eyes had healed after the inflammation that had raged in them and the doctors told me that you were entirely blind and would never be able to see, that my heart bled for you.

You were a little baby then and I had such misgivings when I thought of your future.

"I brought you to several eye surgeons in the hope that something might be done for you. But they all said the same thing. Then I heard of Dr. Bendeke and took you there. He consented to operate, but he warned me that the outcome would be very uncertain.

"For three days I got you ready for that operation, and all three days Dr. Bendeke failed to appear. The suspense was terrible. But I didn't lose hope. There was something about the man that told me I could trust him. On the fourth day he came.

"At first, after the operation, I didn't notice any change in you. Then you began to stretch out your little arms to me and you cried if anyone else tried to hold you. You seemed to take an interest, too, in the little trinkets I gave you to play with. Finally, one day you laughed aloud when I brought out your red coat and hood to take you out, in your buggy. After that there was no doubt in my mind any longer. I knew you could see.

"Dr. Bendeke told me later that the reason he failed to come when he promised he would, was that he had not been able to bring himself to operate those first three days. He said that if the operation had not been successful, it would have meant that your last chance of being able to see was gone.

"It was here where you and I are sitting now," my mother continued, "that I got you ready those days and that Dr. Bendeke gave you your sight."

The fire had burned so low that there were only a few embers left in the ashes when my mother finished telling me the story of my blindness as a baby. I had never heard of it before. I sat silent and motionless.

"Before Dr. Bendeke gave you your sight, I prayed to God that He would let me live so I could care for you," my mother whispered, so softly that I had to strain my ears to hear her, "and you know how generously He has answered my prayers. How greatly He has blessed both you and me. Now I am sure that it will always be well with you."

I sat still, thinking of what my mother had told me. But she was restless, as though she hadn't finished what she had to say.

"It was about the children after I am gone," she said at last "I wanted to speak about them, too. Dorothy is only nine and Robert eleven, and it will be several years before Esther will have finished college and be ready to earn her own living. It will be best if you bring the younger ones to Twin Valley with you, where you are teaching. Your Uncle Enoch and Aunt Elizabeth will be kind to you and will give you good advice when you need it. That will provide a home for the older ones, too, until they have their own."

I promised to look after the younger children and to keep the family together as best I could.

"I don't worry about the little ones anymore," my mother said. "It was hard at first to think of leaving you all. Especially Robert and Dorothy. They are so young and will need a mother's care. But you will love them, I know. It will take your youth, but you will be blessed for what you do someday."

My mother died on the twentieth of May. She was buried beside my father in our family lot in Lakewood Cemetery.

Chapter 4

After my mother died there was the task of getting our things emptied out of the house so we could rent it. The house was a large one and my parents had lived in it for almost thirty years. It was appalling how things had accumulated in that time.

"Let's start with the attic and work down," I told Olga. "Then we'll at least know when we have reached the end."

Just inside the attic stood the cedar chest in which we stored furs and blankets. It was a huge one my mother had brought with her from Norway. Her maiden name, Ingeborg Haugseth, and the date of her marriage 1881, were painted inside the cover. My heart sank as I looked at the chest. I had often heard my mother say that it was carried up in the attic while the house was being built and that it could never be taken down again. It seemed almost like deserting one of the family to leave it behind.

It was even harder to know what to do about my father's engineering library. There seemed no end to the books in it. They were stacked in open shelves at one end of the large room in the attic and were covered with layers of dust. It didn't occur to us that we might call in an appraiser to fix a value on the books and perhaps sell them. It would be too expensive to ship them to Twin Valley, we thought, and, besides, we wouldn't know what to do with them if we got them up there. At last, we decided to burn them. It took two whole days with as Urge a bonfire as we dared to keep going to dispose of them.

We also got rid of, as best we could, the other things we didn't feel we could afford to take along.

It was almost dark when the last load of our household goods left for the freightyards in Minneapolis. The children were with friends where we were going to spend the night. Olga and I were in the house alone.

We swept the floors; and when we had finished, the last of the daylight was gone.

"How about trying all the doors and windows?" Olga asked.

I borrowed a kerosene lamp from one of the neighbors. Olga came with me through the house and tended to the locking up. Our footsteps sounded loud and hollow as we walked over die bare floors.

Neither of us spoke. Our shadows were black and grotesque as they shot over the walls in the rooms we passed. It did not seem

possible that these dark chasms were the pleasant bedrooms which my parents and we children had slept in for so many years. It was not right that strangers should soon be occupying them and calling them theirs.

Downstairs in the parlor the streetlight sent pale shafts over the floor in front of the large window. I remembered that it was exactly at that spot that the caskets of my mother and father had stood, and of my sister Ruth and my Aunt Mary and a cousin of my fathers who was buried from our house.

"Let's hurry," I told Olga. "I can't stand to be here any longer."

We arrived at Twin Valley on the twenty-third of August at about three in the afternoon. Uncle Enoch and Aunt Elizabeth met us at the depot.

"We couldn't get a house for you until last night," Uncle Enoch told us as soon as we reached their home. "We began to be afraid we weren't going to be able to get any at all. It is the only vacant one in town."

"It's pretty well run down," Aunt Elizabeth said, "but when you girls get settled in it, I don't think it's going to be so bad."

"The pump in the back yard isn't far from the kitchen door, so you won't have to carry water more than a few steps," Uncle Enoch went on. "And I know that the water is pure, so you won't have to worry about drinking it. I've spoken to Mr. Ramsey to be on the lookout for a good kitchen range and a coal heater for you that isn't too expensive. You'll have to keep fires going in both of them through the winter. The floors in such old houses are apt to be pretty drafty."

The house wasn't too bad. The pump needed priming, and we were careful to save the last of the water in the pail each time for this. The entrance to the outside toilet was through the barn; but since there were no horses there, it made very little difference except that Dorothy said she would be afraid to go there after dark. I was glad that the four rooms we were to use in the house were all on the first floor and opened into one another. The bedroom was large enough so we could put two beds in there, and Robert could sleep on the couch in the parlor. The attic, which had also been used for bedrooms, was dark and gloomy and we stored whatever we didn't need up there. It seemed queer, especially at night, to be living in this strange house by ourselves.

"You had better stay with us until you are settled," Aunt Elizabeth said to us. "It will be easier for you, and you will be able to work faster that way. We'll come for you in the car for your meals and take you back again."

When we started to clean the house, we were glad we had accepted Aunt Elizabeth's kind invitation. We found that the bedroom downstairs was infested with bedbugs, and it took days before we felt we wanted to put our beds in there. We scrubbed like mad anything that would take soap and water and we sprayed the woodwork with Corrosive Sublimate which Uncle Enoch gave us. After we had done some painting and varnishing and had arranged our furniture in the rooms and hung pictures on the walls and put-up clean curtains at all the windows, the place was more than livable.

There were no lights in the house when we arrived, but Mr. J. F. Heiberg, a pioneer in that part of the Red River Valley who had recently built a power plant near Twin Valley and was installing electric lights in many of the houses in town, came to our rescue. He wired the house and put a single droplight in each of the four rooms downstairs, refusing to accept any money for his services.

"I can scarcely recognize the place," a neighbor told us one evening shortly after we had moved in, "with the bright lights streaming out of the windows and the cozy way you've fixed things up."

But after we had harvested the garden and put our share of it into the little round cellar for the winter, we found that there was still another matter that needed tending to before we could settle down comfortably.

"Something is gnawing at the squash and pumpkins," Ellen said one day after she had been in the cellar. "They have big holes in them and there are piles of fine pulp everywhere down there."

We told Aunt Elizabeth about it.

"Your cellar must be full of rats," she said. "You'll have to do something right away or your vegetables will be ruined."

Again, Uncle Enoch helped us out, this time with Rough-on-Rats. It did the work as well as the Corrosive Sublimate had and soon we were rid of the rats, too.

I worried a great deal that first winter in Twin Valley, especially about the children. I was afraid I was not doing as much for them as my mother would have, had she lived. If they were sick, I

couldn't sleep at night, and whenever Robert or Dorothy cried, I cried with them.

I tried to give them the kind of training I thought my mother would have given them, and I got into the habit of talking Norwegian as she did whenever she wanted to impress something upon us. Then things she said came back to me. I remembered her very words and I found myself using them to the children.

"Hunger is the best cook."

"Self-praise stinks."

"Don't be as undependable as slop water in a trough." "There must be peace in every well-run home." To make these sayings more emphatic, I told the children that our mother used to say them. After a while it was as though my mother were talking instead of me and giving the children good advice even though she was no longer with them.

In March the house we lived in was sold and we had to move out of it just before Easter. Again, we rented the only vacant house in town. Here, too, we found bedbugs and, since there were three bedrooms instead of one, there were many more bugs. We shut off the entire upstairs and slept in the parlor and sitting room downstairs until school closed, when we made a thorough job of getting rid of the bedbugs.

With the coming of hot weather the long, dark shed through which we had to pass to get out of doors from the kitchen became alive with crickets. Uncle Enoch gave us many kinds of poison to try out on them, but they didn't seem to be affected by any of it. If it's true that crickets bring good luck, we should have had plenty of it in that house.

The following November the pump, which like the one at the other house was out in the back yard, went dry and we had to carry water from one of the neighbors' a little more than a block away.

One day, after we had been doing this for several weeks, another of our neighbors, Hermann Klemetsrud, came to call.

"I've seen you carrying water from my brother Ole's place," he said. "That's too hard work, especially for this time of the year. If you'll buy the pipes, I'll dig the trenches for them and connect you with the city water. And I won't charge you a cent for the work."

By Christmas we had running water in the house. The housework seemed easy after that. We scarcely noticed that the faucet was set in the wall of the long and narrow pantry almost down by the floor near the trap door leading to the cellar, and that we had to stand doubled over to tap the water from the faucet.

The second summer we lived in this house we cut the grass first with a scythe and then with the lawn mower. Esther, with the help of some of the young people in town, fixed up a crude tennis court and a croquet ground in the yard. I bought geranium plants full of bright red blossoms for the window box outside the big bay window in the front. The old place took on a homelike atmosphere and we were very happy there.

Ellen married and Esther and Olga were away teaching, and so Robert and Dorothy and I were left alone together in Twin Valley. They were very good about helping me and we got along beautifully.

"Just so you don't tell the kids I wash dishes, I don't care what I do," Robert said to me.

We depended upon the weekends to get much of the extra work at home done. I liked to get up at five o'clock on Saturday mornings so I could have all the dough kneaded and the white clothes rubbed and boiled before breakfast. Robert helped me finish the washing and scrubbed the kitchen floor afterward, and Dorothy did the cleaning of the three front rooms downstairs. By four o'clock in the afternoon the house was spick and span, the clothes dry and in the basket or, if the weather was bad, hanging around the stove in the kitchen, and the kitchen table was covered with freshly baked bread, buns, cinnamon rolls, and perhaps a batch of doughnuts or a cake or a pie. We had also had our baths by this time and were dressed ready to go downtown to do the week's shopping after we had had our afternoon coffee. Saturday evening was free, and we often spent it with Uncle Enoch and Aunt Elizabeth; but we tried to be home early so we could look over our Sunday school lessons, the children's and mine. I taught the young people's Bible class.

Our church in Twin Valley was much less pretentious than the one to which we had belonged in Minneapolis, but I liked it better. I could see what was going on in this smaller one and it was more interesting to be able to watch the choir when it sang and the minister in the pulpit during the sermon. The baptismal service and confirmation and communion seemed more personal now that I could see those who took part in it.

The Luther League met on Sunday nights. I was the president of this for a time. I committed the programs to memory so I could announce them without having to hold the paper close to my face in front of the church full of people. I also looked up the hymns beforehand in my own hymnal and marked them with slips of paper in order to be able to find them quickly during the meeting. I was busy every evening. There were times when I could begin correcting papers and preparing my lessons for the next day right after dinner. Often it was nine or ten o'clock be-fore I could settle down to this. However, I did much of my memorizing at odd moments. I could learn dates in history while I washed and wiped dishes, lists of names in literature during die washing and ironing, and German vocabulary as I was preparing meals or making beds. It was amazing how much time I saved after I learned to combine my schoolwork with what had to be done at home.

Through careful management we got along financially. Uncle Enoch and Aunt Elizabeth gave me good advice and, if things got too bad, let me borrow ready cash. But I had a horror of debt and kept clear of it as much as I could.

Our neighbors who had gardens were generous in their gifts to us. Mr. Meighen, a retired schoolteacher who lived across die street, worked in his garden as soon as it was light in the morning. I was often awakened by hearing his voice through my open window.

"Miss Dahl," he would call, "here is a mess of peas for you." Or he would say, "This lettuce won't stand one more day of hot weather. Come over and pick it before it wilts."

People brought us choke cherries, plums, apples, and rhubarb. I combined these with fruit I bought and canned for the winter. Uncle Enoch's patients from the country frequently paid their bills with cream and butter and eggs and poultry and other meat; and when they brought these in, Uncle Enoch ordered some for me, too, because I could get them cheaper in this way. Just before Christmas I usually bought a hog and a hindquarter of beef. A part of this I left frozen out in the shed, and I canned some of it. I also rendered lard and made headcheese and a kind of Norwegian bologna called *rulle poise.*

In the fall I bought twenty bushels of potatoes from a farmer and a bushel each of carrots, rutabagas, and onions. I ordered flour by the hundred pounds from Mr. J. F. Heiberg, who owned the power plant and was also the miller. I generally bought sixteen cords of green wood and had it sawed and split. Robert, Dorothy, and I piled it first in the back yard to let it dry out and later in the shed for the winter. The pile shrank conspicuously while it lay outside, and I began to doubt the wisdom of this practice and bought the wood already to burn. I used to buy the year's supply of coal while it was the cheapest, just at the time school closed. Doing this meant a tight squeeze through the summer, but I was always glad to see the bin full of coal in the fall.

Robert and Dorothy and I had a lot of fun together in those days. They loved to have me read to them. We even found time for a few pages at noon if the book was very interesting. We rushed through lunch and the dishes and Dorothy watched the clock while I read. "Time's up," she would say, sometimes so late that I had all I could do to reach the schoolhouse before the first bell rang.

It didn't seem to bother the children that I had to hold the book close to my face while I read to them, and I became so absorbed in the story that I forgot I was doing it.

We played and sang at home together, too. That is, the children sang and either Robert or I played the accompaniments. I gave him and Dorothy music lessons, but Dorothy didn't take to music as Robert did. Robert played and sang with such gusto that Dorothy teased him, saying he frightened the chickens below the sitting room window, so they squawked.

Most of our entertainment away from home was either in church or with the students from school. They seemed to like to have me with them and they never abused this friendly relationship of ours outside of school hours by taking advantage of me while we were at work in the schoolhouse. In fact, the older boys, who had been out of school for a while and were back to finish their last year, did much to keep up the fine spirit there was in the high school.

We had scarcely finished the dinner dishes in the evening sometimes when we heard the jingle of bells.

"That's the kids here, for us to go tobogganing," Robert would exclaim, snatching off his apron and hiding it on a hook behind the kitchen door.

"Come on, Miss Dahl," I would hear a voice calling from outside. "We're waiting for you."

It didn't matter that the thermometer went down to thirty or forty degrees below zero. We bundled up and went anyway. As we swooped down the hills east of town, the sharp air cut like steel against our faces. Sometimes we were spilled into deep snowdrifts; but we picked ourselves up laughing and made our way to the top of the hill once more, where we were ready for another trip down.

Everyone in town and people from the country around Twin Valley came to school affairs. The second year I taught there Miss Inez Holm, the eighth-grade teacher, and I put on a little play I had written. We used her room because it was larger than the high school assembly room, but, even so, the place was packed. The basketball games were held in a vacant building downtown, and here there were such crowds that the players were sometimes tangled up in the mob of onlookers.

The year following Robert's graduation from high school, we moved away from Twin Valley. Robert could no longer live there as he was going away to school, and Dorothy would be ready for the university in two years.

"You ought to try to get a better position," Uncle Enoch and Aunt Elizabeth told me. "The school is so small that there is no future for you here."

I applied for a position in the schools of Minneapolis, but I wasn't successful in securing one. So, I accepted an offer to teach at Enderlin, North Dakota. The children went to school in Minneapolis, and we were no longer able to maintain a home where we could all be together.

Nineteen hundred and eighteen was a bad year for me to come to Enderlin. The town was a division point of the Soo Line and, because of the increase in business on the railroads during the war, it was crowded. It was difficult to find living quarters and mine were far from comfortable. I missed the children, too, and worried about them a great deal.

The influenza epidemic broke out soon after I arrived and as a consequence the schoolwork was badly interrupted. The second fall I was in Enderline a streptococcus epidemic which was almost as bad struck the town and the country around it.

My eyes, too, may have had something to do with my difficulty in adjusting myself to the town. I rather felt that they did. I didn't learn to know the members of the school board at all, and before I became acquainted with people my appearance was always against me. The first week the loafers sitting along the sidewalk on Main Street mumbled insinuating remarks about my eyes just loud enough for me to hear, and some ragged little boys shouted at me once or twice when I was on my way to the post office. However, after a short while these annoyances stopped entirely.

I took my meals at The Beanery, the railroad restaurant at the depot. It was the best eating place in town and was run by a fine couple by the name of Mr. and Mrs. Reed. Railroad men of all classes came there: men from the roundhouse, firemen, engineers, brakemen, telegraphers, dispatchers, conductors, the trainmaster, and the division superintendent. Many of them were relatives of my high school students. Since the dining room was seldom used except for special occasions, the regular patrons sat on high stools along counters in the large room. Except for the waitresses I was often the only woman there. The railroad men always treated me courteously and never embarrassed me with any reference to my eyes. I thought them a very fine group of gentlemen. We talked about school and railroading, and I learned many interesting things about the railroads from them.

It was while I was at Enderlin that it began to dawn on me for the first time that my eyes need not be entirely a disadvantage to me in my teaching. Because of them I had suffered so much that whenever I came in contact with anyone in trouble, I wanted to help that person.

"All people have handicaps," Maria Sanford told me, and now I was discovering them among my students.

There was, for instance, the freshman boy who kept bringing bugs and worms to school to frighten the girls. One day he put a frog in the desk in front of him, and when it jumped out at the girl who sat there, she screamed so that she upset the whole high school assembly. I kept the freshman boy after school.

"Why did you do that?" I asked him.

At first, he acted with an air of braggadocio about the whole affair. But after I had talked with him for a while, I suspected that, in his heart, he was embarrassed and even sorry about it.

"You're too much of a gentleman to treat a girl like that," I told him.

During the next few weeks, I tried to draw him out and I found that he had traveled more than most children his age. I encouraged him to tell me and later the students in his English class about the places he had visited. Soon he was bringing pictures for us to see: a beautiful scene from the Canadian Rockies, views of Niagara, and one day a snapshot of Mark Twain's home in Hannibal, Missouri. His classmates were much impressed, and he became much the hero in their eyes.

Then I learned why it was that he had been up to so much mischief. He was very small and slight, and, because of this, he was unable to take part in many of the boys' sports and join them in other things boys like to do. He felt badly about this and as a consequence developed an inferiority complex. To ease his feelings, he teased the girls and tried to show them that he was a tough he-man, unafraid of anything.

Another boy who shoved the smaller ones around in true bully fashion came from a home, so I learned from one of the teachers, where he scarcely ever heard a kind word from one end of the year to the next. Before I tried to draw this boy out, I made it a point of being unusually kind to him and of thanking him for courtesies I had to stretch my imagination to discover.

"It was good of you to hold the door open for me," I told him one day when he all but slammed it in my face.

He looked back at me and scowled without saying a word.

Another time he picked up a piece of chalk and had his hand raised to use it on the coat of a boy in front of him when I took the chalk from him, pretending I thought he was giving it to me.

"Thank you for picking up that chalk before someone stepped on it and crushed it," I told him,

He looked surprised, but I noticed at the end of the morning that he marched out in an orderly mariner without annoying anyone near him.

A week or so later he handed in a rather good paper on The Man without a Country, I praised him before the other students in his class and asked him to read a short portion of it. The boy began to volunteer, and I was amazed at the range of his general information.

"You were wonderful in class today," I told him after we had been discussing A Message to Garcia and he had made some fine contributions to it. "Where did you learn so much about Cuba?"

He beamed.

"My uncle fought in the Spanish-American War, and he told me lots about it," he said.

He became one of my most dependable students in the high school.

There were others I helped, too. I noticed at once the little girl who was hard of hearing, and it was no trouble at all for me to change her seat to a place where she could see to read my lips. When the work of a very good student began suddenly to slump, I knew something had happened and it wasn't long before I got her to confide in me what it was. Her mother, who was ill with tuberculosis, had become much worse and the girl had to do the housework at home and care for the younger children. I told the other teachers about the girl, and we gave her extra coaching so that at the end of the year she made her grade even though she had been absent much of the time.

My heart went out to these young people and somehow, after I had been able to do something to make life easier for them, I felt better about my eyes.

I was fortunate in going next to Harmony, Minnesota, to teach, for the little community certainly lived up to its name.

Most of the homes there were large and painted a snowy white. They were set far back from the street and in summer were almost hidden by the dense foliage of the tall trees in the yards. Everyone in town loved flowers and from early in the spring until the frost came in the fall their gardens were full of them.

At the south end of Main Street, the Lutheran and Methodist churches, both of them beautiful red brick structures, faced each other from high, terraced green lawns. Many women in town belonged to both Aids, and the services at the churches alternated so people wouldn't have to miss either. The ministers took turns delivering the baccalaureate sermons and giving the invocation and benediction at the commencement exercises of the high school graduating classes.

In mild weather on Wednesday and Saturday evenings, when the stores were open late, families from Harmony and the country around brought their suppers to the park, which was located in the center of the town, and they asked anyone to join them who happened to be passing by. It was also a common thing for housekeepers to invite guests home with them to dinner on Sundays, and sometimes I had three and four invitations by the time I had made my way down the aisle to the back of the church.

If there was sickness the women in the neighborhood telephoned to one another to make arrangements to do up the work for the family that was having the trouble. In cases of death, they decorated the church and the grave with plants and flowers they brought from home; they furnished food for the relatives who came to the funeral and housed them if there was not plenty of room in the house where the death had taken place. When there was a marriage, the whole town gave the bridal couple a shower.

There were also certain people in Harmony who took upon themselves special duties, and everyone knew about it and regarded it as a matter of course. Emma Thundale and her mother made it a point to look out for new teachers, although they didn't have anyone in school themselves, and at times there were two or three teachers spending the weekend with them. Mrs. Editor Johnson, who was the first woman in Harmony to vote after woman's suffrage came in, knew every parliamentary law that had ever been written. If you wanted a slip for a plant, you went to Malviny Miller; a choice recipe for any kind of food, to Mrs. Quammen; your fortune told to Mrs. Kirkelie. Any child who wanted anything went to Anna Seem, who was the primary teacher. When she walked through town from the schoolhouse to her home across the tracks on the north side, children of all ages would call out to her, "Hello, Miss Seem. I saw you in church, Miss Seem. I'm going to give you a birthday present, Miss Seem." There was never a Harmony child in a hospital, nor one who had a handicap of some sort or needed any help, that Anna Seem didn't remember in some way.

No one could talk about the school without mentioning Mr. Parry, the supervisor of music. He was a little Welshman who had brought with him to America his Welsh accent and his love of music, and he was already a tradition in Harmony when I arrived. He was at his best in the Christmas program, which the high school and the grades had together in the little, old opera house a block off Main Street the morning before vacation started. He stood between two tall, sweet-smelling evergreen trees, his flushed face framed in a shock of white hair, directing the singing of the boys and girls and himself joining in the Christmas carols as though his very life depended upon it.

Perhaps it was the music in the school as well as the harmonious surroundings that had such a wholesome effect on the high school students. Certainly, the discipline there was beautiful. None of the children was spoiled by having too much, nor was there any real poverty among them. Their attitude reminded me of my students at Twin Valley. However, the town of Harmony was a generation older than Twin Valley; and so, everything in Harmony was more permanently established.

At school and even on the street I began to recognize people more readily than I had heretofore. Perhaps I was unconsciously adopting the short cuts in this as I had learned to do in committing to memory what I taught in school. I enjoyed absolute peace of mind. I roomed with Julia Soum the first year and with Anna Seem the second, and at both places I felt perfectly at home.

But, notwithstanding my joy in my work and my happiness among the people in the town, something was causing me considerable concern. At first, I wouldn't let it bother me. I told myself that it was my imagination, that because I wasn't used to having things coming my way, I didn't have sense enough to appreciate the good when it did, that I was hunting for trouble. But at the end of the second winter, when it came time to think about signing contracts for the coming year and the closing of school, I had to admit that I was facing a reality, and I knew that I would not be returning to Harmony in the fall.

It was my eyes.

Chapter 5

"I wonder whether your mother will mind if I don't leave until Monday?" I asked Anna Seem when we were on our way home from the high school commencement exercises.

"Of course not," Anna said cordially. "We'd love to have you stay longer if you care to."

"No, I'll have to leave on Monday," I told her. "I plan to take the noon bus to Rochester."

"Why, Borghild, you aren't sick, are you? Or maybe you aren't going to the clinic?"

"Yes, I'm going to the Mayo Clinic. It's my eyes. You see, I haven't done anything about them since my mother died. She always saw to it that I went at least once a year."

"Have they been any worse than usual lately?"

I didn't answer Anna. I never talked about my eyes to anyone, and I couldn't bring myself to do it now. I hoped Anna Seem and her mother hadn't noticed how red and inflamed my eyes had been all year, especially the sightless one. The last month or more, even the good eye had pained me so I felt I should scream.

Without any further discussion on the subject Anna told me on Sunday evening that she was going with me to Rochester. She knew the town and the clinic, she said, and it would be much easier for me that way. This was so like Anna that I accepted her offer gratefully.

It was unbelievable that a small town like Rochester could have so many tall buildings and that, early in the morning as it was, the streets were already crowded. Cars were packed along the curb as tight as they would go, and from the names of the states which Anna read on the license plates it was evident that people had come from all parts of the country. We met patients in wheelchairs, nurses in white uniforms, redcaps and bellhops, and well-dressed men and women who looked as though they had money enough to buy out the world.

After breakfast on our way to the clinic Anna pointed out to me places whose signs I couldn't read: restaurants, hotels, cafes; rooming and boarding houses; convalescent homes, hospitals; and, in the center of them all, the clinic.

The girl at the registration desk in the Mayo Clinic asked me whether I had an appointment with one of the doctors there. I told her I hadn't. Then she asked me whether there was any special doctor I wanted to see. I told her no. In what section did I want to go, she demanded next. I didn't know that either, I told her, but I had come to consult someone about my eyes.

The eye section was at the end of a long, narrow, and rather dark hall. Chairs were lined up on both sides and many of these were already occupied. Anna and I took the two nearest to the desk at which a young lady was sitting. I handed her the envelope that had been given me when I registered, and soon afterward she came over to me and asked me to follow her. I was nervous and begged Anna to come with me. We were ushered into a small consulting room.

To my surprise there were many doctors who came to see me there. First, a short dark one looked at my eyes for a long time through a glass, and then a very tall one examined me even more thoroughly. After that still others came, and because there were so many of them and I was so uneasy my impression of the later ones was even more hazy. The routine was familiar to me because I had gone through much the same thing on my visits to Dr. Bendeke and Dr. Boeckmann. But there were many more examinations and they seemed more complicated than those I had had earlier.

At last, I was left alone with the two doctors whom I had first seen. The tall one began to talk to me.

They would be able to do something for me, he said, which would relieve my headaches and stop the inflammation in my eyes. The right one was useless and should be removed, since there was grave danger of it affecting the other one. The sightless eye was disfiguring, too, and an artificial one would greatly improve my appearance.

"Do you really think an artificial eye will look better than the one I have now?" I asked, scarcely able to realize what he was telling me.

"Certainly. I doubt if anyone will suspect that it isn't your own," he said.

"How wonderful!" I exclaimed, my voice trembling. "When can I have it done?"

"We'll have to find out first whether you can take a little ether," he said.

I was sent into a larger and lighter room. Anna couldn't go with me here. There seemed no end to the doctors who came and went So much commotion, I thought, just to have an eye removed.

While I was having examinations and tests, I heard a girl's voice from somewhere saying, "Rush order Dr. Benedict. Rush order Dr. Benedict."

At last, the examinations and tests were over. They had taken most of the morning. I was given an admission card to the Worral Hospital for five o'clock that afternoon.

Anna became panicky when I showed her the card.

"I can't stay alone with you when you have this operation," she said. "Your sisters will never forgive me if anything goes wrong. We'll have to send for Dorothy."

I didn't need to send for anyone, I told her. I had never been so happy in all my life. Didn't she understand? Those surgeons were going to help me get rid of this unsightly eye of mine. I had always hoped and prayed that someday this might happen, but I had never really believed that it could be done.

"I'm so thrilled I could dance a jig right now," I told Anna.

But she looked unconvinced and worried.

"Come on," I said. "Anyone might think you were going to have the operation instead of me. Cheer up. There isn't a thing to worry about. Take me to the swankiest eating place in town. We're going to celebrate."

She was still far from enthusiastic, but she took me to a good restaurant, and we had a fine meal.

At five o'clock we went to the hospital. After I had been put to bed and she came up to the room to see me, she became panicky again.

"Your sisters will shoot me for letting you do this," she said.

Her voice shook as she spoke.

"All right," I agreed at last. "Have a nurse bring me a telephone and I'll call Dorothy."

I got Dorothy at the dormitory on the university campus. She almost collapsed when I told her I was talking to her from a hospital in Rochester, and she insisted on coming down right away. But I convinced her that this wouldn't be necessary and that I would enjoy a visit from her later much more.

I didn't sleep at all during the night. I kept thinking about how it was going to feel to be in crowds knowing that people weren't pointing me out as the girl with the terrible-looking eyes and pitying or ridiculing me because of them. I remained perfectly calm all the time up to a little after noon, when I was put into a wheelchair and taken up in the elevator from the second floor to the fourth. There I was left out in the hall. Men and women in white hurried past me, and some of them disappeared behind the double doors just ahead of me. Red and white lights flashed off and on, and every once in a while, a gong sounded. I began to think about the operation I was going to have and wondered what it would be like. The scalp on the top of my head prickled and something hurt inside my chest. Perhaps it wasn't my eyes after all that had given me my headaches, I thought. I was almost sorry I had come to the clinic.

One of the men in white came over to me and so did a nurse. They wheeled me through the double doors and into a room with a skylight overhead.

It was very quiet. I lay down on a table.

"Sit up a minute, please," said a voice close to my ear. A man in white examined both my eyes.

"All right," he said. "You may lie down again now." Someone put a mask over my face.

"Breathe deeply."

It was a woman's voice this time.

I felt myself choking, but before I could do anything about it, I seemed to be floating in the air and then I didn't know anything more.

I was pretty sick when I came out of the ether. Anna stayed in the room with me that first bad night and for several more. I dreaded to see the house surgeon come near me and I held my breath as he removed the bandages and stirred up the pain again in my eye. But before long I was able to leave the hospital. Anna remained in Rochester with me so she could take me to the clinic every day to have my eye dressed.

One Sunday morning Dr. Gosse, who was taking care of me, brought me into a room where there were two other men.

The one was elderly with white hair and a long white beard, and I knew I had never seen him before.

The other one I recognized at once. He was the tall doctor who told me the first day that I was to have an examination to see whether I could take ether, and I was pretty sure he was also the one who looked at my eyes in the operating room. On both occasions, however, I was so wrought up and excited that I didn't get a clear impression of him at all. Now I saw that he had a magnificent physique; his eyes were so piercing that they seemed to look straight through me, and in his handsome face there was an expression of great power but of the gentlest kindliness, too.

I didn't realize as I sat there that Sunday morning that he was Dr. Benedict, the head of the department of ophthalmology at the Mayo Clinic; that, although he was still a young man, he was a great surgeon and in years to come would rise to be one of the world's outstanding doctors in his field; least of all, that he would become my good friend and adviser and would have a greater influence than anyone else on my life for the next twenty years or more.

"Dr. Benedict, this is the patient you just mentioned," I heard Dr. Gosse say, addressing him.

"Miss Dahl, I'd like to have you meet Dr. Fuchs of Vienna," Dr. Benedict said to me.

While the three of us were talking, several other doctors came into the room. After a little, Dr. Benedict explained to them and to Dr. Fuchs the details of the operation on my eye. It had receded far back in my head almost to the brain, he told them, and so after it had been removed, he inserted a glass ball to provide a cushion that would fill the socket and make the two eyes almost the same size. The glass ball was connected with the muscles of my good eye in order to coordinate the movement of the two.

"That's a marvelous piece of work," I heard one doctor exclaim under his breath as he bent to take a good look at the eye.

"You see," Dr. Benedict said, turning to Dr. Fuchs, "she will have rather free movement in the eye."

"Yes, yes, I see," Dr. Fuchs said, looking at the eye long and earnestly. "That is good. Very good."

All the time I was recuperating at Anna Seem's home in Harmony, I kept thinking about the artificial eye and how I was going to look wearing it. I asked Mrs. Seem every day whether the socket was healing.

"It's getting better," she would say, dropping the medicine into it, "but you mustn't expect too much. Remember that was a serious operation."

I asked her also how the socket looked. Was there a deep hole there? Did she think the artificial eye would be as large as the other one?

"I can't say," she told me, "but the socket surely looks nice."

I was supposed to spend a part of each day in bed, but I was so excited that I couldn't sleep during the day.

"If you would try to rest, your eye would heal quicker," Mrs. Seem scolded me.

At last, the day came when Anna and I went back to Rochester.

Dr. Benedict removed the bandage and looked intently into the eye. Then he went over to a cabinet and brought out several wooden boxes. Inside these against velvet cushions, arranged like rings or brooches in a jewelry store were rows of artificial eyes. There were Hue ones in various shades and also brown and gray ones.

"Let's see," Dr. Benedict said, looking into the boxes and at my good eye. "You need a blue one. don't you?"

He took out several and held them up to my eye. At fast he put back into the case all but one.

I sat tense.

"All right," he said, "let's try this one."

With the fingers of his left hand, he opened the lid of my eye that had been operated on, and with his right one he slipped the artificial eye into the socket. It felt cool at first, and smooth.

"Now do as you did before," Dr. Benedict told me. "Let your eyes drop and then raise them. That's right. Now to the left. Now right." At first, when I did this, it seemed almost as though I had a cinder in my eye. But after I had tried it two or three times more, I didn't feel anything.

"By Jove," Dr. Benedict exclaimed, "that eye even has an expression in it that exactly matches the other one. Now then, take a look at yourself."

He handed me a mirror.

I could scarcely believe that the face I saw was mine. Instead of the unsightly eye, sunk far back into my head and densely scarred, there was now a perfectly normal one that looked exactly like my good eye except that it didn't have a small white spot.

"It's perfect," Dr. Benedict said.

Then he went on to tell me how I should care for my eye. The socket would have to be treated with medicine for several months, he said, before it would have healed enough for me to wear the artificial eye comfortably.

"Even after it has healed," he warned me, "you must take the eye out every night so that the socket can rest, and you must treat it every morning and evening. If you don't, you will be back here for an operation much worse than the one you have just had. Remember, the socket must be kept clean."

Then he explained how I could prepare my own boric acid solution from the crystals, since I would be using this all the rest of my life. Although the hall outside was full of people, many of whom, I knew, must be waiting to see him, Dr. Benedict did not seem at all hurried. He questioned me about my family and my education and how I had gone about teaching. He seemed surprised that I had gotten along as well as I had. He said he thought I would make a sympathetic worker among the blind and he gave me the names and addresses of several people in New York who might be able to give me information about this.

I felt that I was taking too much of his time and I thanked him for all his kindness to me, thinking this would give him an opportunity to dismiss me. But he went right on talking to me.

"One more thing about your eye," he said a little later. "About every other year or so, you'll have to buy a new one. Some people have so much salt in their systems that they can't wear artificial eyes more than a year. But the normal life of one is two years. When it begins to scratch and is discolored, you'll know you need a new one."

"I'll do anything you say," I told him. "Only please let me wear the new eye back to Harmony. I'll promise to put the bandage on again as soon as I get there."

Dr. Benedict laughed.

"All right. I don't think that will hurt any. You'll see that she keeps her word, won't you, Miss Seem?" he said to Anna, who had just entered the room.

I rose to go.

"Wait," Dr. Benedict said. "Dr. Prangen wants to try to fit you to some new glasses."

He took my arm and led me into another office.

"Dr. Prangen, what do you think of our patient now?"

A man at the other end of the room came toward us. He was short and rather stocky, and when he was really close to me, I recognized him at once. He was the dark-complexioned doctor who first examined my eyes the day I arrived at the clinic.

"She certainly looks fine," Dr. Prangen exclaimed. "The artificial eye is so natural that people will think it is the one that has been operated on."

He had me read a chart across the room. I could see only the large F there. Then he turned the chair and tried the one behind me. I did a little better with this one, but not a great deal. After that Dr. Prangen sat down at his desk and wrote something.

"Here is a prescription for new glasses," he said, handing me a small, white envelope. "At first you aren't going to think much of them. But if you are patient and give them a fair chance, I believe they will help your eye very much."

When Anna and I left the Mayo Clinic, I felt as though I was a new person and that I was starting out on a life in a different world.

I stayed with Esther while I was recuperating that summer. She and her family had recently moved to Sauk Rapids, Minnesota, where they lived in a little cottage set off by itself near a wood that sloped down toward the river. It was quiet there and we seldom saw anyone. I was glad of this, for my eye had to be bandaged most of the time and my right cheek was badly discolored from either the eye operation or the extraction of some teeth which one of the examining doctors at the Mayo Clinic had advised.

When I began to feel stronger, I tried to think of what I should do during the coming winter. Dr. Benedict and Dr. Prangen had suggested that I take a year off from teaching, but they hadn't said anything about not going to school. I had for some time wanted to take up graduate work, but I hadn't seen my way clear to do it. I had had one summer session at the University of Minnesota on a small stipend the school board had granted me at the end of my first year of teaching at Enderlin, North Dakota. But the time had been so short that I hadn't accomplished much.

I sent for catalogues from the graduate schools of several large universities, and after studying them I found that Columbia appealed to me.

"I think I'll go to New York," I told Esther one day.

She looked at me.

"What in the world are you going to do there?" she asked.

'I'm going to school," I told her.

She stared.

"You can't do that," she said after a little. "It's only the last week or so that you have felt like anything at all."

"Yes, but I'm improving right along, and Columbia won't open for almost two months."

"If you must study, why can't you go to the University of Minnesota? That's close by, and if you get sick you won't be away from everybody."

"I'm not going to be sick," I said.

When Selmer Ramsey, my brother-in-law, came home for the weekend and we talked the matter over, he agreed with Esther.

"The University of Minnesota is a fine place," he said. "Why don't you want to go there?"

"Because I've spent most of my life in Minneapolis," I told him, "and as long as I'm taking the year off, I might as well go where I can see something."

The only people who were enthusiastic about my attending Columbia were Uncle Enoch and Aunt Elizabeth.

"It's a good school," Uncle Enoch said, "and it will be wonderful for you to have a year in New York City. As for your eyes, if reading and studying hurt them you would have ruined them long ago. Mother and I used to worry about you when you stayed with us here at Twin Valley because you used them so much. But you seem to get along all right with whatever you set out to do and I'm sure you will at Columbia, too. Only do try to take care of yourself. Remember that your health is more important than anything else."

He looked at me with that kindly expression of his that always reminded me of my mother.

"Dr. Benedict and Dr. Prangen didn't say you shouldn't use your eye, did they?" he asked a little later.

"No," I answered truthfully, "they didn't. They only said I should be careful to have a good light when I worked."

I left for New York the last week in September. Ida Twedten, who at one time had taught in Twin Valley, was going to Columbia, too, and we made the trip together.

We arrived at Pennsylvania Station in New York at ten o'clock on Sunday night. Ida Twedten's friends told me of a good hotel just off the Columbia campus. It was The King's Crown and I registered there for the night.

When I was alone in my room, I sat down on a chair to catch my breath. I was in New York. I became so weak all of a sudden that I

was afraid I would faint. There was a pitcher of water on the dresser, and I poured out a glassful and drank it.

"Don't be a baby," I told myself. "You're having the opportunity of a lifetime. You'd better make use of it."

I looked around the room. It was small and modestly furnished, but to me it had an atmosphere of distinction.

"New York," I repeated under my breath.

A telephone book lay on the table beside me. It was the largest telephone book I had ever seen. I took it up into both my hands and balanced its weight against my body. Then I opened it and held it up to my face and tried to read some of the names on the leaf to which I had turned, but I found that the book was so heavy that I couldn't get my eye close enough to see the print. I climbed upon the bed and put the book there, too, and crouched down and dipped my face into its pages just as I used to do on the floor with the books I couldn't handle when I was a little girl.

I tried to think of names of important people I had read about in the newspapers, and as they came to me, I looked them up in the telephone directory. Astor, Morgan, Rockefeller, Vanderbilt. I also looked up the names of authors whose books I had read, and well-known actors and actresses. Some of them evidently didn't have telephones or else they didn't live in New York City, for I couldn't find them. I turned to the D's and there were several Dahls, but no Borghild Dahl.

"Wouldn't it be funny if my name should one day be in a New York telephone book?" I said aloud.

I laughed at myself for being so silly. If I survived the year I would be doing well, I told myself.

It was four o'clock in the morning when I finally shut the huge telephone directory and undressed and put out the light.

After breakfast I had a telephone message from Ida Twedten saying there was a vacant room in the apartment where she and her friends lived. It was a court room with no daylight in it, but I took it on the spot since I was glad to be living near Ida. Most of the girls in the apartment were nurses who were taking courses at Columbia and working part time at the Henry Street Settlement House. They all cooked their meals in the kitchen they shared in the apartment, and they were such a jolly bunch that I became acquainted with them right away and felt perfectly at home.

As soon as I was settled in my room, I decided to go over to Columbia and ask someone about the advisability of entering the field of education for the blind. I was referred to their sociology department on the main campus.

The professors there said that I had been trained for the teaching of seeing children and that ten years of experience ought to have convinced me that I was able to do it. My eyes didn't look as though they were giving me any trouble now, they said, and it seemed to them that the logical thing for me would be to continue with the kind of work I had been used to. However, they thought it might be a good idea to take my master's degree in sociology since that would help me a great deal no matter what kind of work I took up later.

I went away from Kent Hall, where the department of sociology was located, walking on air.

"My eyes didn't look as though they were giving me any trouble now," I repeated to myself.

A few days later I registered as a graduate student at Columbia with a major in sociology. I was told that with close application and by writing an acceptable thesis I might be able to earn my degree in one year. I took a course in economics and one in United States history and I entered Miss Scarborough's class in short story writing to fill out my electives.

My greatest difficulty after I got started with my schoolwork was to adjust myself to my new glasses. I knew I ought to be wearing them, but it took me much longer to read with them and I kept pushing them off and putting on my old glasses while I was studying. The print was much clearer with the new ones, but it was so small that before I could make out the tiny letters, I had to press the book or paper closer to my face than ever. I finally hid the old glasses when I sat down to my books in order to rid myself of the temptation of going back to them. Gradually the print seemed to be growing larger while I was wearing the new glasses and at length, I realized that I was reading much more easily than I had ever done before.

However, wearing them around my room and out of doors was quite another matter. When I looked into space through them, the world seemed to end in curves, and I was afraid of taking a step for fear my foot wouldn't land where I intended it should. But after a while I found myself forgetting to take off the new glasses when

I had finished studying; then I began to wash dishes with them on, and to walk around the apartment. One day in February I was in the elevator before I remembered I was wearing them and, since I was only going to the neighborhood grocery, I decided not to go back for the old ones. I fumbled down the steps leading out of the apartment house and made my way cautiously to the store. Luckily, I didn't have to cross the street and I got back to my room safely.

After that I wore the new glasses whenever I went to this store, and in time the world seemed to straighten out and I became surer of my footing. But even when I was wearing the new glasses all the time, I was nervous on the Columbia campus. There were so many steps there and I was always afraid of falling. I eventually solved this problem, however, by counting the steps along the walks leading to the buildings.

 where I had my classes and also those in front of these buildings, and I tried to remember how many of them there were in each place. Although during December and January the days were so short that it was not very light when I went to my first class in the morning and it was completely dark after my last one in the afternoon, I was fortunate enough not to have a single accident.

All the girls in the apartment were living in New York for the first time and they spent every spare moment they had seeing the city. They often invited me to go along with them and I accepted every invitation because I was wild to go sight-seeing and was afraid to go places by myself. After I had been on several trips, one right after the other, I was completely worn out. So, I began to set out by myself. First, I tried using the Fifth Avenue busses when I went downtown. I couldn't read the signs on the street corners while I was riding on these, and most of the time the conductors didn't call them off. But I could always ask someone to tell me. Once in a great while I met a person who either couldn't or wouldn't hear me when I put such a question to him, but there were plenty of other passengers I could turn to. Sometimes I got started visiting with people in this way and I picked up a lot of information I didn't ask for. After a while, if I had plenty of time, I began to pick out people who looked interesting to direct me, with a view to having a little visit with them; and my bus rides, instead of being sources of worry to me, became pleasant experiences that I looked forward to.

It was a little harder to get on the bus downtown than it was to get off. Most people on the streets were in a hurry, and the busses often swooped down on the corners and picked up their passengers and were off again before I could persuade anyone to listen and tell me what the number of the bus was. But if this happened too many times in succession while I stood waiting, I would start to board the bus myself. If, after inquiring from the conductor, I found it was not going to my destination, I would get off and wait for another. During rush hours this wasn't always pleasant, but by the process of elimination I invariably got my right bus and managed to get where I needed to.

When I walked on the sidewalk, I had to get right under street signs in order to read them, and in crowds this was impossible. So, I found it easier, after I had gotten my bearings in places where I wasn't well acquainted, to keep in mind all the time just exactly how far I walked by counting the blocks.

I couldn't see well enough to depend upon the lights from the towers on Fifth Avenue or upon the other traffic signals; so, I usually attached myself to a group that was making the crossing at the same time I was going to, and I kept as close to these people as I could. I figured that even the most careless driver wouldn't mow down a crowd.

It took me the longest time to get used to the subways. The trains speeded so that I could never see the signs in the stations until the trains had come to a dead stop; and even then, I couldn't unless I happened to be sitting opposite a sign. So, I often had to go out on the platform to read it, and then the train usually left me behind and I had to wait for another one. If several went on the same track it meant I had to ask someone which train to take, and in the crowds this wasn't easy.

One rainy evening I was caught in the subway station at Times Square during the rush hour. There was such a mob that the guards closed the gates to clear the station. But I managed to get home all right. After that incident I knew, I didn't have to worry about getting anywhere in New York by myself.

One day Ida Twedten told me she was going to see a play called Will Shakespeare, and she asked me whether I didn't want her to buy a ticket for me, too.

"Sure," I said. "I've never heard of the play; but if it's about Shakespeare I know I'll be interested in it, even though the cast, as you say, doesn't happen to be an outstanding one."

We sat, as we usually did, in the cheapest seats, which were also the farthest from the stage. I didn't have opera glasses and, even with the new glasses Dr. Prangen had given me, I couldn't see the faces of the actors and actresses, nor even their clothing very well except the color of the dresses the women wore. But at that I saw much more than the time I paid almost three dollars for my seat in the back row of the top balcony at the Metropolitan Opera House at a performance of Parsifal, when I couldn't see the stage at all. At Will Shakespeare I was sure I missed many of the finer gestures and other points that helped the rest of the audience to understand the story better. But I heard everything that was said, and I enjoyed the play immensely.

After I went back to teaching, I told the students in several of my classes about the Anne Hathaway I had seen on the stage in New York. I said she was an actress no one seemed to know anything about, and I had forgotten her name, but that she certainly played her part beautifully.

One day a boy in one of my English classes came into my room and I could see he was greatly excited over something.

"Miss Dahl," he told me, "I found a book down at the public library that had a lot in it about the play Will Shakespeare you have been telling us about. The author of it is an English woman named Clemence Dane, and the actress who took the part of Anne Hathaway was Katharine Cornell."

Of all the sights I saw in New York the art galleries at the Metropolitan Museum impressed me the most. This wasn't because I was especially interested in art or knew how to appreciate it. But ever since I was beaten by the freshman drawing course at South High School, I had wanted to do something to make up for it. I wondered now whether, if I tried hard, I couldn't learn to understand at least a few good
points in about a dozen pictures by recognized artists.

Without telling anyone what I was doing I began to make trips, as often as I could find the time, down to the Metropolitan Museum. Sometimes I came just after it had opened in the morning and stayed all day. First, I spent hours walking dose to the walls of the galleries, going from one painting to the other in order to pick out

a few on which I could concentrate. Then I read descriptions of the pictures themselves in catalogues and books of art, biographies of the artists who had painted them, and discussions on the times in which the artists had lived and the schools of art they represented. I also bought good-sized colored prints of the paintings I had selected, and tried to find in them points that were discussed in what I had been reading. When I returned to the galleries, I looked for these same details in the large paintings. At first when I stood close to the pictures in order to be able to see what I was trying to find, I lost the perspective. So, after I became familiar with the paintings I walked backward very slowly away from them, always keeping in mind what I ought to be seeing. After I had reached the place where I was pretty sure that I was depending entirely upon my memory and my imagination, I went up closer to the pictures again. I did this over and over with each painting I was studying.

At last, I began honestly to enjoy going to the galleries. The harmony of the colors in the pictures, the stories they told, and the way they made me feel while I stood looking at them reminded me of beautiful music I had heard and of great books I had read.

Some years later, after I had returned to the Middle West, I visited the Institute of Arts in Minneapolis, and I spent several hours in the galleries there.

"I like this picture the best of your whole collection," I told the attendant who was standing near me.

"I should think you would," he answered dryly. "That's Titian's Christ and it cost the Institute a pretty penny to buy it."

In February I had a long talk with Dr. Giddings, my adviser at Columbia. He told me he was recommending me for a European scholarship. I was much surprised and thrilled to think he considered me worthy of such an honor, but even with his recommendation I didn't think for a minute that I stood any chance of getting it.

A little later I was told to have my credentials sent to the appointment bureau. Columbia University would make the application to the American Scandinavian Foundation for me. I was happy about this, too, and I collected the material they asked for; but still I had no real hope that anything would come of it.

Then one sunny morning in April one of the girls in the apartment came into my room. She had a newspaper in her hand.

"Did you know," she asked me, "that your name is on the front page of the New York Times today?"

I thought she was joking, and I told her so.

"It's true," she said, pointing to one of the headlines.

There it was. I and nineteen men from all parts of the United States had been awarded fellowships for the coming year to the three Scandinavian countries. Mine was to Norway.

While we were still discussing the good news a letter arrived from the American Scandinavian Foundation formally notifying me of my appointment.

It was the happiest moment of my life.

But after I had come down to earth and the first excitement of hearing about my good luck had passed, I began to worry. Suppose the people of the Foundation should find out how bad my eyes really were? That I had only 4/60 vision, and that only in the one eye? What good would it do me that the artificial one looked perfectly normal and deceived people on first sight?

A few days later I received another letter from the Foundation asking me to come to their offices in New York for a personal interview. I was so frightened that I kept postponing it.

All of a sudden, I realized how silly I had been about the whole affair. I would go up to the offices of the Foundation and act natural, and then, if the people there in the course of the interview found that I wasn't the kind of person they wanted to send abroad, I would just have to become reconciled to it. I had certainly had plenty of practice in being a good loser.

Everything seemed to go well up at the office of the Foundation. Mr. Creese, the secretary, was more than cordial. We went over the kind of studying I would do in Norway, and he gave me a few hints about occasions when I would be expected to dress formally. I had never owned an evening gown, so I was thankful for the information. Then he told me a little about the difference I would find in the European standards, and he warned me that it was very important for an American girl to remember at all times that she was representing the women of her country and that they would be judged by her behavior while she was abroad.

The conference seemed to be over. I rose to go.

"By the way," Mr. Creese said in an offhand manner, "you mentioned in answer to the question about your health that you

had had some trouble with your eyes, but that it had not hindered you from doing your work."

It was as though I had been shot. Everything around me started to whirl, and the instant darkness and the buzzing in my ears warned me that I was going to faint.

The next thing I knew I was lying on the floor. A woman was bending over me. She said she was Miss Hanna Astrup Larson, the editor of the American Scandinavian Review.

"I don't usually faint," I heard myself saying. "It's only because I'm tired. I guess I've been working too hard on my master's thesis."

Miss Larson was very kind. I looked as though I needed a rest, she said. I was very thin. A year in Norway would be good for my health. She always gained in weight while she was there, she told me.

There was no further mention made of my eyes.

Just before leaving New York, I received a beautiful certificate which stated that I had been made a fellow of the American Scandinavian Foundation for being a distinguished student in sociology and that I was entitled to a year's study in Norway.

The fellowship provided for a stipend of one thousand dollars, but, as it turned out, the value of the Norwegian crown was so low that year that it amounted to almost double that sum.

In June I had a master's degree conferred upon me in absentia by Columbia University.

Chapter 6

It was like entering fairyland to walk down the gangplank of the Norwegian-American liner Bergensfjord and step on the pier at Oslo. So this was the country where my grandmother lured the cattle home from their wanderings with magic incantations and charmed into docile friendliness the pads of wolves that came down from Finland and prowled over the mountains in Osterdalen, where trolls kept themselves hidden under waterfalls and made the rivers roar, and Wise Knute foretold evens which would take place in the distant future. And it was here my mother and father grew up and had their courtship and married before they migrated to America. It didn't seem possible that I was actually setting foot on Norwegian soil and that I was about to realize the dream of my life.

I stood watching passengers from the boat being met by family and friends. On the lapel of my heavy brown fall coat, I displayed in plain sight the bow of orchid satin ribbon that Uncle John in his last letter to me had suggested that I wear so he could identify me. I knew how poor I was at hunting out people in crowds and I remained standing where I thought he couldn't miss me.

"Are you Borghild Dahl?" asked a pleasant voice in Norwegian near me. "If you are, I am your cousin—Ellen Haugseth."

A middle-aged woman dressed in green held out her hand to me and shook mine warmly.

"Father has a taxi for us," she said, still speaking in Norwegian.

Before we had reached it, I saw a rather small man, in build very much like Uncle Enoch, come toward us. He was holding out his hand to me.

"Welcome to Norway, daughter of my beloved sister Ingeborg," he said. "I hope you had a good voyage over the Atlantic."

He, too, spoke in Norwegian. When I came up close to him, I could see he had the same kindly expression about the eyes that I loved so much in both my mother and Uncle Enoch. He looked exactly like his picture that had stood for years on the mantelshelf in the parlor of our home in Minneapolis.

Tante Sina was waiting with afternoon coffee for us at home in the apartment. We had had no picture of her at home, so I had no idea of what she would be like. She was very tall and thin, and her long black dress and white apron made her look even more so. She wore silver-rimmed spectacles which sharpened the expression in her eyes, her brown hair was but faintly tinted with gray at the temples, and in her cheeks was a warm glow that any American girl in her teens might have envied.

The four of us sat down to a little tea table in the parlor.

"Welcome to our home," Tante Sina said, "and may you have many happy days here with us in Norway."

She raised her glass of liqueur to her lips as she spoke, and so did Uncle John and Cousin Ellen. The liqueur was so strong that I choked on it and asked for cold water.

"It's true, then, what I have heard about America," Uncle John said, smiling. "Among our countrymen over there, they really practice prohibition."

I felt the glances of all three fixed upon me. Tante Sina and Cousin Ellen were kindly but formally polite. Uncle Jolin seemed to be thinking aloud.

"You resemble your father's people, I see," he said as he sipped his coffee.

A little later when the tea table had been set into the corner and Uncle John was enjoying his pipe, he told me how beautiful my mother was and how I had not inherited any of her beauty. There was no malice in what he said, and his manner was so gentle that I couldn't feel hurt.

A few days later he said to me, "You are absolutely haggard and so stoop-shouldered, too."

So, he and Tante Sina set about fattening me up, and a good job they did of it. I drank cream and beer and ate rich cheese and bread with layers of butter on it; fresh fish, meats, and vegetables; and many other nourishing foods. When I grew stronger, Uncle John made arrangements for corrective exercises which I took from an expert in gymnastics. Before he and Tante Sina relaxed their efforts, I had straightened up, so I was no longer stoop-shouldered, and I had gained fifty pounds.

"Now you are beginning to look like a real Norwegian," Uncle John said approvingly, "and a womanly woman. That is much better. When you came here you had the sharp, dark features of the American Indian with not a graceful curve in your make-up."

Uncle John had the idea that people in America, it didn't matter from what European or Asiatic or African stock they had originally sprung, would eventually acquire the traits of the American Indian. He was so thoroughly convinced o' the correctness of his theory that no amount of argument on the subject could change his opinion.

He also had very pronounced ideas about higher education for women. He believed that it lessened their charm to study too much, and that in the long run, even though they might attain fine positions in their fields, years of schooling were a detriment rather than an advantage to them. These sentiments, which he expressed very freely, bothered me considerably.

One day when I had become well acquainted with Tante Sina, I couldn't refrain from mentioning to her what was on my mind. We were alone, having our mid-morning tea together at a little table drawn up to one of the dining room windows.

"It's really too bad, Tante Sina," I told her, "that I should have been the one of Uncle John's nieces to come over here from America. He would have liked my sisters so much better. They look much more like my mother and are not such bookworms as I am."

Tante Sina set down her cup and looked straight at me.

"Oh, I guess you don't have to worry about what your uncle thinks about you," she said a little dryly. "He doesn't approve of higher education for women in general. But when it comes to his own flesh and blood it is a different matter. It is perfectly ridiculous how he boasts about you to people when you are not around."

I was amazed, for that very morning Uncle John had delivered a lecture to me on what he termed my lack of natural refinement in speaking. He objected to my broad Osterdal dialect and the bourgeois inflection of my voice. I must have picked up these unfortunate mannerisms, he told me, over in America from some untutored Norwegians who had come to the home of my parents. Tante Sina's eyes had flashed fire at that remark, and she had spoken rather sharply to Uncle John.

"I know that your sister Ingeborg was a fine and cultured woman," she told him. "But that she couldn't speak the dialect of the community where she was born and brought up—that you cannot make me believe. And that is exactly the kind of Norwegian Borghild speaks, only she reads so much that she has worn off the sharpest edges of the Osterdal dialect. You, yourself, Father, lapse into the same kind of language whenever you become excited."

Pretty soon Uncle John began doing little extra things for me, and dropping hints which showed we were real comrades. He brought me to the depot or to the wharf whenever I was to leave the city on

a little trip. He escorted me to the theater all decked out in full evening dress, carrying a silver-mounted cane. He was really a very distinguished-looking little man, only an inch or two taller than I was. He had a fine shock of white hair and a carefully combed white beard that resembled Bernard Shaw's. Uncle John also accompanied me to church and talked to me by the hour about Norway and the Norwegians: their folkways, their history, their literature. Two or three times a week he went to the library, from which he brought home armfuls of books. Both he and Tante Sina were great readers and we discussed together the books we all three had read.

I think Uncle John was sorry about my eyes, too, although he never made any mention of them to me directly. He could not help knowing, of course, how close to my face I had to hold things to see, since I did a good deal of reading around the house while he was there. He often spoke of my mother's beautiful eyes and how her lovely character shone out through them.

No one else in the family made any remarks about my eyes, other, except the wife of one of my cousins. She said that, after gaining in weight, I looked well and that I really would have had fine, regular features if it had not been for my eyes.

But even though there had been nothing very different about them, my eyes would have set me apart in Norway by the very fact that I wore tortoise-rimmed glasses over them. These hornbriller, as they were called, were just coming into style there and were worn almost exclusively by Americans. Since it was rather unusual to have glasses in Norway at all, my eyes were the first thing people noticed about me.

They looked at my tortoise-rimmed glasses when I walked on the streets. They mentioned them in write-ups about me in the newspapers. They talked about them in addressing me directly.

'I'd have a deuce of a time making love to a girl behind such binoculars," one real Norseman told me jokingly.

But Oslo (Kristiania then) was certainly a good place for anyone who couldn't see very well. There I met with almost none of the inconveniences that usually bothered me in a strange city, or in any city for that matter.

The streetcars were painted a bright bluish-green and even to me were visible at a considerable distance. Their huge signs were down on the level of my eyes, and as I stood on the corners of the narrow streets, I could read them easily: Sagene Ring, Grefsen, Majorstuen. Many of the conductors were women, who shouted at the top of their voices the names of the stops long before we came to them.

I didn't have any trouble finding the places where people lived, either. The house numbers were in large black letters on white oval plaques in such conspicuous places on the buildings that I couldn't miss them. Since the buildings were always right out on the sidewalks, I could read the house numbers as I walked along the streets.

As for being run down on the streets of Oslo, it just couldn't be done. The horns on all the automobiles were shrill enough to waken the dead and there was positively no speeding. During the dark season, from October until April, every animal drawing a vehicle had to be belled. My bedroom window was above a court where a procession of heavy wagons started out every morning; and while it was still as dark as midnight outside, I was awakened by the loud ringing of the bells of the horses and the clattering of their shoes and the rolling of the wagon wheels over the pavement. Even though people in Norway noticed my eyes right away because of my glasses, this didn't make any difference in their attitude toward me. When I met them for the first time, they treated me naturally just as they might have done any foreign visitor in their country. And they were more than cordial and hospitable toward me.

I was invited to become a member of the Norwegian Association of University Women, and there I became acquainted with many leaders among Norway's women. It was here I met Dr. Ellen Glaeditsch of the chemistry department of the University of Oslo. She was brilliant and interesting and had been a coworker with Madame Curie for many years in her laboratory in Paris. Dr. Glaeditsch was a recognized authority on radium throughout the scientific world and had received a doctor's degree from Yale University in America. With all her greatness she was one of the most modest people I have ever known. A few years after I had been in Norway, she was elected president of the World's Association of University Women and traveled in many parts of the United States. While in America she accepted an invitation to come to speak to the school where I was teaching, and she acted as though she, instead of my students and me, were the one honored.

The American Ambassador to Norway, the Honorable Laurits Swenson, was also very friendly toward me. He included rue in a party which he gave at the American embassy, a stately mansion that had once been the home of the Nobel family, the donors of the Nobel peace prizes. On another occasion some of us Americans who happened to be in the country were invited by him to tea on board an American man-of-war anchored in the Oslo fjord. I was also a guest on the Norwegian battleship Tordenskjeld at Horten. By special invitation I attended a banquet of the workers of the Young Men's Christian Association of Northern Europe, and I was an honor guest at the annual banquet of the Norwegian branch of the American Scandinavian Foundation.

I became acquainted with many other people of influence: Halvdan Koht, the great scholar and authority on foreign affairs; Hulda Garborg, the writer; Johan Bojer, well known in America for his books The Great Hunger, The Temple, and The Last of the Vikings; Betsy Kjelsberg, the inspector of factories, and her successor, Aaslaug Aasland; and Dr. Christine Bonnevie, the great Norwegian biologist.

Mr. Haugen, the national commissioner of education, was my adviser during my stay in Norway and he made many of my appointments for me and saw to it that I was introduced to people I should know. Through him I met executives in Norway's motion picture industry, prominent figures on the legitimate stage, professional people, government officials, leaders in industry, men and women important to big business, and many well-known men in Norway's maritime life.

I was invited to speak before organizations in Oslo and elsewhere: farmers' clubs, rural young people's organizations, the Y.W. and the Y.M.C.A., school children from the primary grades through the Gymnasium, the Norwegian Association of University Women, industrial groups, church groups, private groups.

Most of this speaking I did in Norwegian. At first it was rather difficult for me as I had to think in English and then translate what I wanted to say into the Norwegian. I couldn't see well enough to use notes, of course, and sometimes I couldn't find the right word to say fast enough. But in time I spoke Norwegian almost as naturally as I did English.

During the school year I was formally matriculated at the university with a class of cadets, and I was the only girl in the group. Thus, I became a full-fledged Norsk Akademiker. Uncle John told me that this was a signal honor for a foreign-born woman and that he was very proud of me. I couldn't believe my ears when he said this.

On the seventeenth of May I sat in one of the reserved seats directly under the King's and Queen's balcony at the royal palace to view the parade of the school children of Oslo in celebration of Norway's independence day.

During this excitement I felt like Cinderella at the prince's ball. It seemed too good to be true. I was afraid that the clock would strike twelve and that all the festivities and all this grandeur would be ended.

"It's a lively fellowship student America has sent over to us," the dignified elder Morgenstierne of diplomatic fame said to me once when I was laughing at his wit, unaware of his identity and reputation for reserve and stateliness. "You don't look as though you have bothered your head with too much studying or that you have a care in the world."

Yet this Norway with all its festivities and its grandeur was not the Norway of my dreams. It wasn't the fairyland where my mother and father grew up and my grandmother Haugseth lived her charmed life and where trolls made the rivers roar.

I would have to go up into Osterdalen to find that Nor-

way: Osterdalen, the great eastern valley that extended along the Swedish border from Hamar to Trondheim: the giant valley that was made up of many smaller ones and was studded with high mountain peaks and that held in its lap the mighty river Glommen; the valley of fertile farms and the richest timber in the country.

In November I had a letter from one of my cousins inviting me to come up to Osterdalen to spend the Christmas holidays. There was to be a wedding, she said—a second cousin of mine was to be the bridegroom—and there would be other family gatherings.

I read the letter aloud to Uncle John.

"You'll freeze to death up there," he said.

"You don't know how cold it was in Minnesota in America," I told him. "At Twin Valley, where Uncle Enoch lives, it was fifty degrees below zero sometimes."

"But you didn't climb mountains in such a temperature," Uncle John insisted. "Half the communities up there are inland, and the only way you can reach them will be in a sleigh drawn by a little mountain horse. I advise you to wait until June before you go up into Osterdalen."

But I wouldn't be persuaded to give up the trip. I could stand as much cold as my mother and father had been able to, I told myself, and my grandmother Haugseth, too. Uncle John was beginning to treat me like a baby.

I left Oslo about a week before the holidays. My cousin met me at the station at Tynset in Osterdalen and took charge of me after that. My godfather, who had returned to Norway ten years earlier, lived about fifteen miles away. She had planned that I was to spend Christmas Eve with him; but when on the morning of the twenty-fourth it was fifty-five degrees below zero, she said it was senseless to go. Brydalen, where my godfather lived, was one of the most isolated communities in Osterdalen. I would have to cross a high mountain to get there, and I would freeze my hands and feet and maybe more on the way. However, when my godfather sent Morten Rusten on a motorcycle for me, she gave in. It wouldn't take Morten more than fifteen minutes to make the trip, she said, and if I was well covered up, she didn't suppose I would freeze in that short a time.

It was noon when Morten came. He had attached a little box sled behind the motorcycle where I was to sit. This was full of wraps my godfather sent over for me: his fur coat to put outside my own; ragger, long, heavy, woolen stockings that came up to my hips and were pulled over my shoes; Finn shoes of fur to go outside the ragger; and a fur robe. To these my cousin added shawls, blankets, and another fur robe. I felt as snug as a baby in its crib after my cousin finished tucking me in the box sled.

The motorcycle slipped easily up the mountainside. The air was so sharp, and we went so fast that I almost lost my breath. We had been out for only a few minutes, it seemed, when Morten told me we had almost reached the top and would be going down again very soon. We would make much better time then, he said, and meanwhile he hoped I wasn't minding the cold too much.

All of a sudden, the motor began to chug and then to miss, and the box sled was being jerked by the chain that held it to the motorcycle. Then our speed slackened, and the chugging grew fainter. Finally, all sound from the engine ceased and we came to a dead stop. Morten still sat on the motorcycle, but from the peephole in the red knitted woolen shawl that covered my face I could see that he was bending over it.

"Is anything broken?" I asked, thoroughly frightened by his manner.

"That's what I'm trying to find out," he said shortly.

I got out of the sled and tried to walk over to him. But my wraps were so clumsy and heavy that I could scarcely move.

"I'll push," I told him, "and you pull as hard as you can. Maybe we can get it going again that v/ay."

Both Morten and I worked as hard as v/e could, but the engine remained as dead as a doornail. At last, completely exhausted, we straightened our backs and stood still.

I tried to think. I knew I couldn't run with all these clothes on. I couldn't even walk and make any headway. And it was so cold, and I sweated so much when I tried to push the motorcycle that I didn't dare to take off any of the clothes.

"Run for help," I said at last. "I'll stay here."

He looked at me as though he thought I had taken leave of my senses.

"I can't do that," he said. "Do you realize that it will be hours before I get back here? You'd be frozen to death by that time."

"Hurry up," I said. "It's the only thing we can do."

Then I laughed.

"Aa du kan skratle? (And you can laugh?) You American girls are certainly queer," he said.

After Morten was gone, I climbed back into the box sled and covered myself with the shawls and blankets and robes. But they had become chilled, and I soon felt the wet clothes next to my body stiffening like ice clamps about me.

"This won't do," I told myself, getting out of the box sled once more.

But now I couldn't see the narrow path anymore because it was already beginning to grow dark, and so I didn't dare to take one step away with the box sled.

"You'll have to bundle yourself up again," I told myself, "or you'll freeze standing still out in the snow."

Inside the sled and under the covers once more, I felt myself growing colder every minute.

"You fool, you've got to move," I said to myself. "Didn't you hear what Morten said?"

There wasn't space enough inside the box sled to move anything but my arms.

"That won't do you any good," I said.

Then it came to me that if I let my feet dangle outside the box sled, I could move them freely. So, I began pulling my legs up and down, first one and then the other, and I found that this rocked my body, too. Soon I felt the heat return inside of me and I thought I wouldn't have anything to worry about anymore. But then I began to be tired, and my movements slowed down. Finally, I had to drag myself to keep going.

I wonder if singing would make it any easier?" I asked myself.

"Glade jul, hellige jul (Silent night, holy night)," I began.

The time in this song was perfect for the movement of my legs and for a little I forgot how tired I was. I could remember only the first verse in Norwegian and I sang that about twenty-five times. Then my voice gave out.

"I can't keep warm moving my mouth anyway," I said hoarsely.

My glasses had thick wads of hoarfrost on them, and they were beginning to freeze on my face. Although I was afraid of losing them, I took them off and wiped them on the red knitted shawl. While they were off, I looked around me. I was appalled when I realized that it was much darker—that night had already set in.

It was harder not to be frightened in the dark. Even though I hadn't been able to see anything behind my frosted glasses, I hadn't had the helpless feeling that stole over me now. It was dangerous for me to move because I could so easily slip and fall out and lose myself.

I had stopped moving and it hurt me so that I dreaded the thought of starting again.

"I'll just rest for a while," I said.

But as soon as my body was quiet the icy grip of my wet clothing tightened around me.

"Come on, come on," I told myself. "Get going again."

I had no idea of how long I had been struggling to keep warm when my poor feet simply refused to move another inch.

"Try with your arms," I commanded. "That's better than nothing."

In some way my hand became entangled in the red knitted shawl, and I knocked off the glasses. I made a dash for them, but I couldn't find them. I began to cry.

"I can't stay here any longer and live," I said, wiping my face on my shawl.

I felt something sharp sticking into my ear, and after I had fumbled around for a while, I discovered it was one of the bows of my glasses.

"You'll be all right yet," I said, laughing and crying at the same time.

But now there was a cold steel rod where my spine had been.

"Up and down," I said, beginning to move my feet very slowly once more. "Up and down, up and down," I repeated. "Up and down. Up and down."

I thought of the wolves that my cousin had mentioned that morning. There were hungry packs of them, she said, that had come down from Finland and were prowling up on the mountains in Osterdalen. If only I had asked my mother about what my grandmother Haugseth did to make them docile and friendly, my mother might have known and told me. That was always the way with me, I thought. I never knew enough to take advantage of things when I had them.

"You couldn't even scare off a rabbit if you tried," I told myself bitterly.

My legs weighed tons by this time. It took ages just to get ready to move each one, not to mention how long actually to do it.

Then the idea came to me that if I lifted my feet with both my hands the feet wouldn't seem so heavy, and so I grasped my left leg and began pulling it up in the air. I lost my balance and almost fell out of the box sled. I felt the perspiration trickle all over me.

"It's so dark now that if you get only a foot away from the sled you're lost," I whispered after I had recovered somewhat from my fright.

I began to feel drowsy.

"Don't you dare stop moving, no matter how tired you are," I said angrily. "You know what it means when you get sleepy in this cold."

A pleasant warmth came over me. I tried to tell myself that this was because I still kept moving, even though it was centuries

between each time my feet went up and down. But my stiff body made me suspect that it was something different.

"Well, you got what you wanted," I said. "Christmas Eve in Norway. Up in the fairyland of your dreams. In Osterdalen. But there aren't any trolls under the rivers to make them roar now. They're all frozen."

I shivered.

All at once I pushed the wraps from me and stood up in the box sled. I pulled off my glasses and strained my eye as hard as I could to look into the darkness.

"Morten," I called. "Morten, Morten, Morten."

But only the eerie howling of the wind answered me. "I'm not going to die," I cried, even louder than before.

"Do you hear me? I'm not going to die."

I couldn't remember much after that until I was in my godfather's home in Brydalen. After I had been revived, they told me that when Morten returned to Tynset without me my cousin was almost out of her mind. She called the girl at the telephone office, and the telephone operator put in a general alarm through the whole valley. People started out on motorcycles, on skis, in sleighs, on horseback, and on foot to look for me. It took five hours for help to reach me, and then the whole countryside assembled on the mountaintop. No one expected to find me alive.

But, strangely enough, only my heels were frozen and these not too badly.

Long after I had returned to America and had almost forgotten the incident, my cousin wrote me from Osterdalen saying that people in that part of the country now reckoned time according to the number of years it was since the Christmas Eve when the Dahl girl was left sitting on the mountaintop.

The next time I went up into Osterdalen, it was June. Everything was different up there then. The weather was balmy and there was life everywhere.

One evening my cousin's daughter, Anne, invited me to go with her to a picnic up on Morna, a near-by mountain peak. It was broad daylight when we started out at nine o'clock. Although the going was steep, we ran almost the whole way. Anne was familiar with the path we took, and I followed close behind her. Peculiarly enough, I wasn't in the least afraid of falling. After hearing her take each step above me, I touched with my hands the stones she had

just left and so I knew exactly where my feet should go. Above the evergreen woods that covered the foot of the mountain, the air was freer, and I felt so light that it seemed to me that I could fly if I tried hard enough.

On both sides of our path small mountain torrents rushed down through narrow ravines which Anne said had been frozen over only the week before. Several little waterfalls tumbled over precipices near us and startled us with their sudden roars as they rushed pell-mell into the valley.

It was about midnight when we reached the top of Morna and, although the sun had set, it was still light enough to read. Anne unpacked the lunch, and we sat down on a boulder and munched flat bread and goat cheese and sipped black coffee.

The cuckoos began to call to one another from the mountain peaks that surrounded us. First, we could hear only a few, but gradually the volume of their song increased until there was a whole chorus of them; and yet we could make out the separate calls and answers as the birds courted their mates. I inhaled deep breaths of fresh air. It was so clean that it seemed that it blew every impurity out of my lungs. As I looked into the distance, which appeared to me like a blurred stretch of purple and gold, the sun came stealing from behind a high ridge toward the east.

"Sweden is right over there," Anne said, pointing in that direction. "I can see the mountains across the Norwegian border."

Although I knew I wasn't seeing what Anne pointed out to me, I realized I was sitting in the midst of some of the most beautiful scenery in the world. Even a blind person could sense that, I told myself.

At last, my stay in Norway was over. It had been a glorious adventure. I grieved to leave Uncle John and Tante Sina and all the others who had been so kind to me. I wept when I looked in vain from the deck of the steamer for Norway's distant shoreline.

But the pain of parting with the dear people I had left behind was lessened by the thought of what lay ahead of me. I could scarcely wait to set foot on the firm earth of the United States once more. I was thrilled to be returning to my homeland and at the prospect of going back to work. I was a new person now. I could scarcely remember my old self—the stranger who only a little more than two years back left Harmony so discouraged that life had scarcely seemed worth living.

I wasn't afraid to try anything anywhere now.

Chapter 7

I wanted very much to teach in a college and so I stopped off both in Chicago and in Minneapolis to interview the managers of several teachers' agencies.

"We'll have a good position for you by the second semester," they told me. "If not in a college, at least we can promise you one in a good-sized high school."

It was heavenly to hear the managers of the teachers' agencies tell me this. I knew they looked at me very carefully during the interviews and they must have been satisfied with my appearance. It was unbelievable that I wouldn't have to worry any more for fear my eyes would prevent me from getting into the work I wanted.

I went to teach in the high school at Bismarck, North Dakota, on the following New Year's. The position wasn't exactly what I wanted, but I needed to earn money and so I was glad to accept it. An English and French teacher had married during the holidays, and I took her place.

I liked Bismarck from the first. I had two very fine men to work with at school: Mr. Saxvick, the superintendent, and Mr. Bublitz, the high school principal. They were real educators and gentlemen in the finest sense of the word.

I liked my work, too. Teaching as I did in a small classroom, I had no discipline problems. I could use all my energy trying to make my classes interesting, and my two years of travel and study gave me fresh material to present to them.

The prospect of teaching French bothered me somewhat.

It was a long time since I had studied the language; and although I had attended a few lectures given in French both at the Nobel Institute in Oslo and during the World Conference of University Women there, this could scarcely be considered a preparation for teaching it. I knew, therefore, that I should have to do some strenuous studying to keep up with my classes. They were fairly advanced in reading, especially the second-year students, and in order to commit to memory most of what they covered I should have to work hard, at least on vocabulary.

I started memorizing my French lessons the first night I had my textbooks. For weeks after that I lived in an orgy of French. I went to sleep in French, and I woke up in French. I washed, dressed, and combed my hair in French. I ate, drank, and left the table in French. I went to school, greeted my students, and conversed with

the teachers, all in French. That is, I did it first in English with them, and then later told myself about it in French. I read the French assignments for my classes until I caught myself reciting parts of them in public and caused myself no end of embarrassment.

On looking over the storeroom where the high school texts were kept, I found that the only classic left for my sophomore English class was a set of Scott's The Talisman. I was disappointed about this; for I didn't consider The Talisman suited for intensive study in class at all, at least not for high school sophomores. However, there was nothing to do but to use the books and make the best of it.

I read The Talisman many times before I commenced to present it to my class. After that I put forth my very best efforts to make it interesting to my students. The results were unbelievable. The boys and girls loved The Talisman. They discussed it with great enthusiasm during the recitation period. They drew pictures of scenes from it at home and brought these to school to show their classmates. They also sewed costumes for dolls to represent characters in the book. They carved miniature buildings and weapons out of wood. And when they had finished the study of the book, they put on a play based on some of what they considered the most interesting episodes of the novel.

My experience with The Talisman was very heartening. What wouldn't I be able to do now with a classic that I really liked and one that was suited to my students?

One of the extra jobs that fell to my lot at school was the coaching of a play that had already been selected but for which there was no director. Old Days in Dixie, it was called; and, as the title suggested, it had the romantic atmosphere of the old South. The art and music departments looked after the stage settings, the costumes, and the music, so my only responsibility was the speaking parts. As it turned out, the girl who played the role of the blind woman stole the show. She groped about the stage fumbling for things and acting exactly like one who couldn't see. She perfectly imitated the very gestures and mannerisms of a blind person, people said. They marveled that a girl so young and with perfect sight could have thought of doing these things. I was the only one who guessed the reason why.

Since I had so recently returned from abroad, I received requests to address many organizations in the city: the Rotarians, the Hi-Y's, the Sons of Norway, church groups, and societies among the teachers and children in the public schools. I accepted all of these invitations and enjoyed meeting the people I came in contact with, in this way. Speaking in Norwegian, which was really a foreign language to me, had been excellent practice, for I had had to learn to express myself in precise words. Appearing in public as often as I had in Norway had also given me self-confidence.

But the thing that made it easiest for me to address strangers now was the realization that my eyes were no longer so ugly that people noticed them at once. The first day I stood before my students in the classroom at Bismarck, I didn't have to wonder what they thought of my eyes. Although even now they were far from beautiful, they were a vast improvement on what they had been. After almost three years I still felt a thrill whenever I picked up a mirror and looked into the pair of eyes that greeted me in my reflection. Of course, I still had poor vision. But I was used to that, and I could largely overcome this difficulty by being very careful of my actions in public and by committing anything and everything to memory in my room, where no one needed to know about it. But I had been helpless before with that densely scarred eye of mine. All I had been able to do about it was to try to develop my personality as best I could in the hope that people would eventually like me in spite of the poor impression my first appearance made on them.

Everything went so well at Bismarck that I became very hopeful about the future. As soon as I could, I would establish a little home of my own, I thought. Since the old home had been broken up, neither Dorothy nor I had had any place where we really belonged. We had a suitcase here, a trunk there, and boxes of our possessions everywhere. When we needed our things neither of us was able to locate them. I decided now that I would make a few household articles that we could use when we settled in our home. That would at least be a start I bought material for towels and began to hem them by hand. I found my sister Olga had been right when she said once that I could see well enough to sew if I were willing to exercise enough patience.

I received a much bigger salary at Bismarck than I had ever been able to earn before. At the end of the year I was given a substantial increase, too. But I was offered a position at Watertown, South Dakota, where a part of my work would be in a junior college, and so I accepted this offer. It was with real regret, however, that I left the many friends I had made during my short stay at Bismarck.

I realized as soon as the superintendent at Watertown had taken one good look at me that I had not found favor in his eyes. All the anguish of the years caused by my inferiority complex and my feeling of futility came surging back over me. Only now it was in multiplied form because I had thought that I had left all that behind me. The man made no comment to me. He did not visit a single one of my classes. He offered no suggestions. But in his estimation of me I knew I had failed and that there was not a single thing I could do.

In the spring I received an offer to go to Sioux Falls. In this position I would have only college work. It would be in English and Journalism. The salary was attractive. And I heard that Sioux Falls was the largest and the finest metropolis in the Dakotas.

The prospect of going to a new place didn't trouble me very much. I was somewhat uneasy after my late experience at Watertown, but it had not affected my determination to forge ahead. With the removal of so many odds as I had had against me, I wasn't going to give up now.

I knew I was going to love Sioux Falls the very first morning I arrived there. I was a total stranger, but I had no feeling of loneliness. Since no one knew me, I could browse about for days undisturbed, and whenever I stopped to transact some little item of business I was treated with the greatest friendliness.

The college, although an old institution, had recently undergone a complete reorganization. It had changed from an academy and normal school to a four-year college of liberal arts. There was much to be desired in the way of buildings, library facilities, and other equipment, but I learned during my first week on the campus that the school could boast of as fine a student body as could be found anywhere.

From the first the college became an altar at which I worshiped. The promotion of its future and the welfare of its students were a sacred trust—became a religion with me, in fact. It was natural that it should be so. The school had been founded by early settlers of my own nationality. Its ideals were the ideals of my faith. A good percentage of those who shaped its policies were ministers of the gospel in my own church. I believed in the work I was doing. I was bringing good literature to the attention of my students and trying to help them to appreciate it and love it, and I was convinced that good literature could have an uplifting influence on their lives. I believed in South Dakota—that it was a state with a great future. Most of all, and this last grew on me, I had faith in the young people who day after day came into my classroom.

In the college I taught various courses in English: the survey of English and American literature, Chaucer, the Elizabethan drama, Shakespeare, the romantic period and the Victorian age, the novel, the short story, modem drama, freshman rhetoric, journalism, and a course for high school teachers of English. I soon discovered that my students had missed out on much reading they should have done earlier, and so I began to make plans for offering a course in children's literature for teachers in the grades. In preparing for this course, I received the hearty cooperation of book agents in our territory, and of educators in the city and around the state.

"Always give the children the best," I told my students after I had begun to offer this course in children's literature. "They will appreciate the classics if you present them simply and clearly enough."

There were many opportunities outside of school for me to make my classwork interesting. I encouraged the students to be on the lookout for worth-while pictures at the theaters, and sometimes I reviewed for them the books on which the screen version had been based. Whenever a play on the legitimate stage came to town, we talked it over for weeks beforehand. and the second balcony was crowded with my students on the night it was put on. Because I had been unable to appreciate grand opera myself the first time I went to New York, I wanted to help my students to enjoy those that were given in Sioux Falls. We discussed the stories of Carmen, Hansel and Gretel, Faust, and others that came to the city, looked up the lives of the composers, and found out anything else of interest about the opera that we could.

The students were so much on the alert to take advantage of everything that I learned as much from them as they did from me. The journalism class, especially, kept their eyes and ears open.

"Huey Long's in town," one of the boys told me one day. "I'm going down to get an interview. I'd like to find out whether he's the sort of fellow the papers make him out to be."

The student came back the following afternoon.

"He's worse," he told me. "I spent almost an hour with him in his hotel room and he talked all the time. He said he had made every public official in the state of Louisiana and he's branching out to Washington next."

Other students came back with interesting stories about such celebrities as Jeanette MacDonald, Marion Anderson, Carl Sandburg, and Theodore Roosevelt the second.

Every moment I had to spare I read: newspapers, magazines, and books. I discovered that I had to be on my toes to keep abreast of these eager young people.

In recitations at school, for the sake of appearance, I had on the desk before me anthologies or other textbooks out of which the students read. For my own lectures I never referred to a book or a note of any kind during the thirteen years I was at the college.

I became so interested in good reading that I talked about books wherever I went. People began to associate me with them and to ask my opinion concerning them. Pretty soon I was reviewing books before small groups to which some of my closest friends belonged. After accounts of these reviews appeared in the Sioux Falls Argus Leader, strangers asked me to speak. I gave book reviews at the meetings of church groups of all denominations, professional and social groups of men and women, study clubs, societies in other colleges in the city and the local high school; and the public-school teachers invited me to come to their buildings to speak to the children in the grades. The children learned to know me and called me by name when they met me on the streets.

For two years I reviewed a different book each Monday morning over radio station KSOO of Sioux Falls, and I received hundreds of letters from people who heard me give them.

One day the announcer asked me to wait for a minute before beginning my broadcast as he had something he wanted to say first to the radio audience. I didn't try to listen to him because there was always more or less advertising to be done and, besides, I couldn't usually hear what was said from the booth where he spoke. However, this morning the door must have been left ajar, or something else happened, for I was startled to hear my name spoken.

"Miss Dahl," said the announcer, "is sitting here in the broadcasting room as usual without a book or a scrap of paper of any kind to use while she gives her book review. To see and hear her doing this week after week is one of the greatest marvels I have experienced since I took up radio work."

I was so surprised that I almost had to give up my book talk that morning. It hadn't occurred to me that anyone had noticed that I spoke without notes, and I was certainly not anxious to have anyone's attention called to the fact. With me it was simply a matter of survival not to use them.

All my book reviewing within the city I did without any thought of receiving payment for it. But when I was offered money from out-of-town audiences, I accepted what was given me. The books cost me considerable and there was often expense connected with transportation. Sometimes I received as much as twenty-five dollars for a single lecture. I became curious to know what I could do with the extra money I earned in this way, and so I put it aside in a fund by itself. When this had gone on for a while, I found that I had enough to buy a chest of sterling and a dinner set of Wedgwood.

I also accumulated a good-sized library. I received many books as gifts from book agents and publishing houses. Sometimes the groups before which I was to review books gave me copies of the ones I used. Often the bookstore presented me with those I reviewed over the radio. And I bought all I could afford and more. I was chosen one of three or four people in town to do book reviewing for the Book Review Guild of America. It fell to me to review Gone with the Wind when it came out. The messenger brought my copy at eleven o'clock one morning and, since there had been some delay in sending it, I was asked to have my report on the book ready by the next day. It was fortunate that I had no classes for twenty-four hours after that, for I spent all of them reading the book. However, by eleven o'clock the following day I had read the book and had my written criticism ready to go to the typist. I had read all night; but although I had had to hold the huge book so close to my face that the lashes of my left eyelid brushed the pages as my eye raced over them, the eye was not inflamed or even tired when I finished.

By the spring of 1932 I had saved enough money to make a down payment on a home for myself. Dorothy had accepted a teaching position in the East, but she would return to Sioux Falls for her summer vacations and perhaps sometimes at Christmas. The house was only a very modest little bungalow, but it was adequate for our needs. Dorothy, whose training in home economics had made her a model housekeeper, helped me pick out the furnishings for the house and made it cozy and homelike.

The summer we planted our garden the state of South Dakota had one of the worst droughts in its history, and for many years in succession after that there was scarcely any rain. Month after month the wind blew in terrific gales, burning up everything that it swept over.

The city of Sioux Falls got its water supply from deep wells, and so the people in town were allowed to sprinkle their lawns; but most of the homeowners became so discouraged at the continued dry, hot spell that they finally gave up the struggle and let their yards become parched and brown.

Dorothy and I had the sprinkler going from early in the morning until almost midnight every day to keep the trees and shrubs and grass we had planted from dying.

One Saturday when it seemed that the wind was burning up everything it touched, Mr. Monserud, who had helped us set out the garden, came over to see how things were.

"You'll have to wrap wet burlap around the trunks of the trees and the hedges," he told me, "and spread cheesecloth over your lawn. Nothing can live under this scorching sun, and the wind blows like flames out of a bonfire."

The first year that the lilacs tried to bloom on the bare sticks of the back hedge, the flowers came out looking like dirty bits of shabby gray astrakhan fur.

But in spite of the drought our yard began to show improvement. We got rid of the gopher holes and the molehills with which the place was filled when we came. Everything we had planted grew; and after a while the ground had a soft covering of tender, bright green grass, and the spindly branches of the hedges were almost hidden by small, fresh leaves, and there were tiny patches of shade under the little trees. The yard looked clean and attractive and, in the evening, when the wind played through the spray of water from the sprinkler, it was cool and pleasant to sit out there. We bought lawn furniture and after that we formed the habit of eating our supper out of doors when the sun had gone down. People, dropping in, told us that they wouldn't know there was a drought while they were at our place.

The students at school, too, enjoyed coming over. I didn't have an office at the college and so I had my private appointments with them at home. Often these conferences started out with a little lunch. I let the young people help me prepare it and afterward, when the ice had been broken by the informality of the kitchen and we were seated in comfortable chairs in the living room, it was perfectly natural for the students to confide in me and tell me what was on their minds. I learned that the drought was even harder on the farmers than on us city people and that the parents at home were making heroic sacrifices to keep their children at school. I marveled after the stories I heard that there was money enough so the students could be there at all.

"We haven't had a drop of water on our place since early last spring," one girl told me. "Dad has to haul even the drinking water in a tank for ten miles. Mother wrote me in her last letter that she has to measure the water for the clothes washing by the cupful."

"The sandstorms out our way are terrible," another one said. "It gets so dark from them that the folks have to leave the lights on all day sometimes. Mother stuffed the windows with cotton to keep out the dirt, and even then, it got so bad that she took down the curtains and put them and the rugs away in trunks. It just wasn't any use trying to keep them clean any longer. She says she goes over the floors and the tables and chairs almost every hour and then things are gritty."

"Dad shipped off the cattle last week," one of my boys told me. "He simply couldn't stand to look at the bones sticking out of them any longer. He kept a milk cow, but I don't see how he's going to feed her."

One evening a boy who worked in a laundry downtown came directly from work to my home to discuss his term paper. I invited him to have supper with me out in the back yard. He was hot and tired when he arrived, but after we had eaten, he seemed rested and comfortable.

"Gee, it's swell out here," he said, looking around admiringly. "I wish I could set that sprinkler for just one day on our Chinese elms

at home. Mother carried water to them for years and they had just gotten real pretty."

One Sunday in May, Laura Oberg, my old college chum, who had married and was living in the western part of the state, visited me, bringing along her husband arid her two children. Clair, her little son, was born after the drought had begun, and in their town, there had been almost no vegetation since then.

While we older people were busy talking, Clair came running into the house all excitement.

"Just think, Mother," he cried, "Borghild has grass in her yard. Do you hear, Mother? Grass. She's got grass."

Then he turned to me.

"Will you please let me step on your grass?" he asked politely.

As the educational standards in the state were raised, it was increasingly necessary for the teachers in the public schools to improve their educational qualifications. During my first years at the college, I began to teach extension courses in the evenings especially for their benefit. For years I continued to teach these extension classes at the college without any thought of compensation for my work. The friendships I formed meant much more to me than money could have done. My extension students were, with very few exceptions, mature people whom I greatly enjoyed; educators, many in executive positions; businesswomen; nurses; and a few ambitious housewives.

I, too, tried to improve my education. For three consecutive summers, while Dorothy was still teaching at the college, she and I drove East in our own car to take summer courses at Columbia. These trips with Dorothy meant much to me since she understood the difficulty with my eyes and helped me in innumerable ways when I was trying to see things.

One year I, with two other professors at the college, was granted sabbatical leave to continue with graduate work. I had been happy over my other two scholarships, but this one in some ways meant even more to me. I had now made good as a college professor, and I was leading the dignified life of any other successful man or woman in the academic world.

I planned to spend the year in Nev/ York studying at Columbia. I had rented out my home in Sioux Falls and was all ready to leave when I received a jolt. The authorities at the college sent word to me that they found they could grant only two stipends, and these would have to go to the two men who had been granted sabbatical leave with me.

I had been so proud of my sabbatical leave and my stipend. The money meant much to me, but the recognition of my efforts meant even more. Then the old familiar sore spot inside of me began to ache again. Yes, I supposed. As usual, at the bottom of all the trouble lay my eyes.

The college authorities finally reconsidered, and I was granted my stipend. But the thrill that I had first felt over my year's leave was gone.

After this incident I decided I would go places with my doctorate. If my eyes had had anything to do with the college authorities' change of heart, I would show them that I could accomplish as much as anyone with a pair of good eyes. If being a woman was against me, I would prove that my sex wouldn't be downed either. I would literally stull myself with knowledge.

After coming to Columbia, I went to the office of Dr. Wright to make arrangements for mv examinations in German and French. He was friendly and we sat talking informally for a while. In the course of our conversation, he began to talk to me in German, and then he changed to French. I responded in both languages. After we had kept this up for a time. I said that I should like to make arrangements for a definite appointment to take the examinations.

Dr. Wright smiled.

"Vous avez passe les deux examinations." he said. "We do not worry about people who speak German and French as
you do.

But with the Latin I didn't fare so well When I took this examination I had to translate from a book, and I was nervous and embarrassed because I had to hold it so close to my face. The letters whirled around me on the pages, and I continually lost my place. I passed the examination, but I wasn't proud of the impression I made.

Shortly after these examinations were over, I received a written communication notifying me that I had been elected to the English Graduate Union of Columbia University, which is the honor society for students taking advanced work in English in the graduate school there.

I was so happy that I sat down and wept. This unexpected honor more than made up for my earlier disappointment.

During that entire year I did my level best, albeit unknowingly, to commit bibliolatrous suicide. From six in the morning until three the next morning, on Sundays and holidays, I poured over books as if I were bereft of my senses. I begrudged the time it took for my baths and the washing of my stockings and my underwear every morning at three. I became impatient if I had to stand in line at the cafeteria.

I spent weekends with Dorothy in New Jersey. It was a little confusing at first to change from the tubes under the Hudson to the Broadway subway after I had left Hoboken. Before I was used to the route, I allowed myself an extra half-hour for getting lost down there. But even this experience gave me a certain feeling of independence, for I always managed to muddle out of the labyrinth 2nd stumble upon the outlet marked Broadway Subway. After that it was easy to find my way along the narrow passage to the station at Cortlandt Street. Once on the train, all I had to do was to count the stops first on the local and then on the express until I reached One Hundred and Sixteenth Street, where Columbia University was located.

This commuting to New Jersey became such 2 cut-and-dried affair as the year wore on that the depots at Hoboken and Dover, the trains, and the subways all became my study rooms. I didn't mind who saw me holding my books up against my face because no one knew who I was. Besides, I had only one thought in mind. That was to forge ahead in my work at the university.

Such insane conduct could, of course, have only one outcome. I had a nervous breakdown. It happened on the day when I was beginning to take my oral examinations.

As a consequence, I didn't receive my doctor's degree.

It took half a year of loving and intelligent care, first from Dorothy and later from Uncle Enoch and Aunt Elizabeth, to bring me back to health once more.

After I had recovered, I went back to work at Sioux Falls.

I was glad to be teaching again, for I felt I was being useful. And it seemed to me that being busy and useful were the greatest blessings that anyone could enjoy.

Chapter 8

Most people of middle age look back to one particular year as their annus mirabilis. When their affairs have turned out so well that Browning's song "God's in his heaven: All's right with the world" seems to have been written especially for them.

The school year 1938-39 was like that for me. It wasn't that the events in themselves were so outstanding, but rather that I had the feeling that now at long last I had caught up with good fortune.

My finances were in better shape than they had ever been. Each new position I had taken had always meant a substantial increase in salary. Besides, at the college I was earning extra money by teaching nine weeks of summer school every year; and of late I was also being paid for my work in the evening classes during the winter. In all, my income averaged almost five times as much as it had when I first started out on my career as a teacher.

I was perfectly comfortable physically. The bungalow, on which only a small mortgage remained, was well equipped. Dorothy had bought an electric refrigerator, a vacuum cleaner, and a washer, and I had only recently bought an electric range with a time clock on it so I could set my dinner in the oven when I went to school at noon and find it ready to serve on my return. Dorothy and I had given each other an electric clock with Westminster chimes, and this meant much to me because I had to walk right up to other clocks to find out what time it was. Every year we added some comfort or convenience until my housekeeping had become mere child's play.

I had even embroidered in cross-stitch on linen a dinner set of a dozen napkins and a large tablecloth. This had given me immense satisfaction. I certainly didn't have to worry any more that my eyes were going to prevent me from doing everything I set my mind on. At last, the drought had broken in South Dakota, and the rain had done wonders for our yard. The trees and hedges and the grass were at the stage where they needed very little attention, and this I could give them before I left for my classes in the morning.

The schoolwork was pleasant and easy. I had taught so long (twenty-five years in all) that I had accumulated a great deal of material which I knew by heart and could use offhand in my teaching. I had leisure enough to read and store up more information for the future. At school the librarians put on reserve the reference books that were listed in the outlines I made for my classes and handed to them at the beginning of each semester, and they provided me with any books I needed for my own use.

My own private library now included more than a thousand volumes. I had made a hobby of collecting certain kinds of books; my Shakespeariana compared favorably with any in the city, and I had good reference material on journalism, the novel, the short story, and the history of English and American literature. I was proud of my Norwegian-American collection and of my autographed volumes and first editions. For ten years I had been gathering clippings and recently had them filed in carefully marked envelopes in a filing case.

For the first time in my life, I felt I could hold my own as far as my personal appearance was concerned. I had ceased to worry about the slight scar on my left eye and the difference in size between the two eyes. I could afford now to dress better than I had ever done before, and my position at the college demanded this. I had a standing appointment at a beauty parlor where the girls knew me and took pride in making me look well; and on special occasions when I was to speak before large audiences, Olga Moore, one of my closest friends in the city, always made it a point to come over to help me with my make-up and to see that everything was all right.

My success as a teacher and as a public speaker had given me poise and self-assurance that was valuable to me in meeting people. I had made a great many friends in the city and throughout the state. In my mail I received almost daily letters from former students. Some of these expressed their appreciation of what I had done for them as a teacher and mentioned their application of the philosophy I had often expressed in class: that all honest labor was worthwhile and could be made dignified if one put one's best into performing it.

I had been at the college for thirteen years. During that time, it had grown from a struggling institution to one of the foremost in the state.

My life was very full, and to me it seemed immensely interesting. Although I was but dimly conscious that anything was wrong, and less willing to admit it, it occurred to me, nevertheless, that I wasn't seeing as well as I should.

Whenever anyone came over to play cards, I got into the habit of pulling up to the table two large reading lamps because I had caught myself confusing hearts with diamonds, and spades with clubs. At the wedding of two of my former students I was disgusted to think the bride had wasted her

own finery and that of her attendants in a church that was so dark that no one could see the bridal party either as it marched down the aisle or after it had stopped at the altar. I couldn't understand, either, why people were beginning to have such miserably poor lights in their homes.

I dusted the furniture three and four times right in succession on cleaning day just to make sure that anyone dropping in wouldn't think I couldn't see to do it well. I blamed myself for being careless when sheets became entangled in the washer and were so badly torn that they couldn't be used any more. And I told myself that there was no sense in always being in such a hurry that I was forever tipping cream bottles in the refrigerator. I scolded myself for leaving fringes along the sidewalks and around the trees out in the yard, telling myself that I must be getting lazy now that the work out there was so easy. However, I felt better about this when the grounds at our place were awarded a first prize in the city garden contest.

Although I wouldn't admit, even to myself, that these things had any bearing on my eyesight, nevertheless I wrote for an appointment with Dr. Benedict and Dr. Prangen at the Mayo Clinic at Rochester for the Saturday following the closing of the summer session at the college. That would be on the fifth of August.

My last class at school was over at ten-thirty in the morning. I had had a fine group of young people to work with and it gave me a lonely feeling to say good-by to them. The last thing I did before leaving the building was to auto-graph several copies of Glimpses of Norway which the students had brought along with them for my signature. This was the little book I had written about my stay in Norway while studying on my American Scandinavian Foundation fellowship.

The day outside was perfect. There was a hint of early autumn in the air, probably due to the smell of ripe, dry grain and upturned earth from (he first fall plowing. As we drove across southern Minnesota, Dorothy and I told each other that we couldn't have had better weather if we had ordered it ourselves. We were in high

spirits at the prospect of our little vacation before, school opened again.

We went to Harmony first to visit with the Seems, and they accompanied us on Saturday morning to Rochester. We were making it a real holiday. Mrs. Seem had packed a basket of lunch and we were going to have a picnic at noon in the park. My appointment at the Mayo Clinic was for nine o'clock and I would probably be all through with the examinations of both doctors long before it was time to go to the park. If, however, they decided that I needed new glasses, we could easily postpone the picnic until later in the afternoon. We had all day to enjoy ourselves.

And then the blow fell.

"When you find that your vision is entirely gone, come back to us and we'll see what we can do for you."

I wasn't sure that I had heard correctly what Dr. Benedict had said. I couldn't believe my cars. The meaning of his words was too dreadful.

"Tell me," I said, trembling. "How bad is it? You don't have to keep the truth from me. I'm no baby."

"No. You're no baby. I've known you too long to think that of you."

My heart almost stopped beating, but I managed to assume a fairly calm manner.

"Are you trying to tell me that I'm losing my sight?" I asked.

Dr. Benedict weighed his answer carefully.

"Go back to your home in Sioux Falls," he said slowly, "and put your affairs in order there."

I looked at him questioningly.

"No matter what happens," he went on, "I am confident that you will be brave enough to carry on."

"Dr. Benedict, do you mean to tell me that I'm going to be entirely blind?"

Again Dr. Benedict chose his words with much deliberation.

"There is a cataract in your eye," he explained to me. "which will have to be removed. Such an operation will be accompanied with great risks. When I begin operating on your eye, there is no telling what I may find there or what will come out of the eve while the cataract is being re-moved."

"Won't I be able to see at all?"

I was sitting in Dr. Prangen's office in the chair I usually occupied while being fitted with glasses. Dr. Benedict and Dr. Prangen and another doctor I didn't know were standing close beside me.

"God can't be so cruel as to take away her sight."

It was Dr. Prangen who spoke. But his voice was so changed that I scarcely recognized it.

I tried to pull myself together. I mustn't faint or shed tears or even cry out. If I did, it was hard telling what might happen. There was nothing heroic about this self-control of mine. I was just too much stunned to realize ye: what was happening to me. Perhaps, too, it was mv lifetime habit of trying to hide my real feelings that wouldn't let me show these three gentlemen how thoroughly frightened I was.

"If this is to be the last time, I'm to see either of you." I said, turning to Dr. Benedict and Dr. Prangen. "I had better take a good look at you."

I gazed into the faces of these two great surgeons who, during the last twenty years, had become both benefactors and friends to me. There was some further examination of the eye.

"It won't be long."

Dr. Benedict said this in a very low voice to Dr. Prangen but being on the alert to what was going on, I heard him.

This remark so completely unnerved me that I couldn't be sure afterward what happened during the last part of the consultation. I understood that I was to go home and wait until I wouldn't be able to see any more. And I was under the impression that this would happen sometime during the fall.

We had our picnic in the park and then we drove downtown because Anna Seem and her mother wanted to do some shopping. I said I preferred to stay in the car because I had a headache. Dorothy started to go with the Seems, but all at once she changed her mind and came back to me.

"Dorothy," I said when we were alone, "Dr. Benedict told me that I am growing blind, that very soon I shan't be able to see at all."

"Oh, Borghild!"

That was all she could say.

But the cry we had before the Seems returned helped a little. Dorothy powdered my face for me when she saw them coming down the street so they wouldn't notice that anything was wrong.

During the days and nights which followed, I couldn't think of anything but that I was growing blind. What kind of person would I become, I asked myself, groping around in the dark?

When I was a little girl, I had been afraid of the dark. My mother used to leave a light burning so I wouldn't be frightened when I woke up. After I was older, I overcame this fear. But now it returned to me, worse than it had ever been. I wanted to scream when I shut my eye and felt the blackness around me.

Then one night I had a dream. I dreamed of my mother.

She was sitting beside me on a green bench in the little park across the street from our old home in Minneapolis. Her head was bent forward slightly as she stitched on some soft blue material. I sat watching her without moving because I wasn't sure whether she knew I was there. I had just made up my mind to tell her when she looked up at me. In her eyes there was the most wonderful expression of love I had ever seen. Even during my mother's lifetime, she had never looked at me like that.

"Do you know," she said, selecting the exact words she used so often when she wanted to encourage me, especially after I was old enough to understand what she told me, "those of us who are not able to see as well as other people must dare to do things. We must have patience and be willing to work harder than those who can see better than we can. And we must believe we can do what we set out to do. Then, if we always keep these things in mind, we cannot fail."

She stroked my cheek caressingly and kissed me just as she used to do whenever I came to her for comfort after someone had made a thoughtless remark about my eyes and wounded my childish feelings. In her eyes, now, there was that same expression of tender compassion which I had seen in them so often when she looked at me years ago.

After I was awake and knew I was in my own bed and in the dark, I could still feel the gentle touch of her hand.

"Yes, but that was when I could see," I argued aloud. Her presence was so real to me that I kept right on talking to her even though I realized that I had been dreaming. "There's a world of difference between being able to see, even though it's ever so little, and trying to go on living in the dark."

I lay there unable to go back to sleep. I went on thinking of my mother, and I began to cry softly into my pillow. I was a grown woman now, but I needed my mother more than when I was a little girl.

Dorothy and I together went over carefully my visit at the Mayo Clinic. I tried to remember exactly what took place during my consultation with the doctors there. The first part of the interview was clear enough, but by the time it was almost over I was so nervous that the last part of it was only a confused memory.

My good eye was now almost without any vision at all because of a cataract in it. I was sure of that much. Also, that the dense scars on this eye made the removal of the cataract very dangerous. Apparently, Dr. Benedict thought there were other complications, too. He said this when he told me he didn't know what he might find after he had begun operating. Certainly, my chances of seeing after the final eclipse had set in were not very good.

There would have to be a period of waiting before the eye would be ready for the operation. During this time what little sight remained in the eye would gradually disappear. Dr. Benedict had said something about having to steel his nerves for the undertaking, and I knew he dreaded it. There was also the question of how the eye would heal after the operation. Very likely two or three operations would be necessary if the first one was at all successful.

After Dorothy and I had had this talk together, and I could face squarely what lay ahead of me, I somehow felt better. No matter how black things looked, it wasn't going to make matters any better by whining about them, I told myself.

I tried to think of something I could do to take my mind off my troubles. After all, I wasn't the only person in the world who had had to face blindness. And I knew that there were those who had met the actual calamity with courage and grace and had gone on leading useful lives.

But what could I do? How was I to carry on as Dr. Benedict said he knew I would?

Why, of course! My writing. It was queer I hadn't thought of it before. Perhaps this was the very time for me to realize my lifelong ambition. All summer I had been working hard on a Norwegian-American novel, but I hadn't really made a business of it. I had had to do my writing in the afternoons after my work at the college was over, and I was always tired when I began. The career of a writer wasn't made as easily as that.

The first rough draft of my novel was almost finished. Hazel Thorne, one of my extension students, had generously offered to type it for me just as Violet Bakkene, another of my students, had done with Glimpses of Norway. The thing for me to do now was to complete that first draft right away so Hazel could get at the typing.

But if I should lose my sight, it wouldn't do, in the long run, to depend on others for my typing. I'd have to learn to do that myself. All right. I'd start at once.

First, I decided I had better commit to memory the letters on the keyboard.

"Z x c v b," with the left hand.

"N m, comma, period, oblique mark," with the right one.

That was the lowest keyboard. Now the second one.

"A s d f g," with the left hand.

"H j k I, semicolon, and the cent mark," with the right one.

After I had learned these so I could repeat them without hesitating, I worked on the upper keyboard. Then there were the extras on the sides, and the changes possible by using the shifts on the lettering and the signs for the numerals and punctuation. I went over and over these details and tried to stamp them on my memory.

Next, I began to place my fingers in the position recommended by a book of instructions I found. The touch system on the typewriter would be invaluable for a blind person, I knew. As I recited to myself my typing lessons, I wondered how I could have been so wasteful of my time while I had been able to see. But I put this thought aside immediately, for it wasn't going to do me any good now to be sorry about mistakes I had made in the past.

After a while my persistence began to have results. I was able to find the keys without looking at them. I kept right on memorizing everything I could think of about the typewriter. If all these technicalities were firmly fixed in my mind before I lost my sight entirely, I could manage the practicing later. My sense of touch would come to my rescue then. I would use my sense of sight thriftily as long as it lasted.

Chapter 9

Since Dorothy would have to return to New Jersey to teach, she decided to take me back with her. We would store our furniture and rent the house because I had been promised a year's leave of absence.

It wasn't easy to leave the little place. Everything in the house and the yard had some close association with my life during the last thirteen years. The end table standing by the davenport and the mirror in the bathroom and a beautiful green vase were left by friends who had a housewarming for me shortly after I moved into the house. The father of one of my students made the stepladder stool that was steady enough, so I dared to climb up on it to reach things on the top shelves of the cupboard. Dorothy had braided the hall rug and had given me for a birthday present the brown and white copy of Hoffman's Christ that hung in the living room.

It was hardest of all to leave my books. Every volume had a story connected with it: pleasant meetings with book agents in the territory and cordial associations with publishing firms by mail; book reviews before interested groups of men and women and at the radio station; conferences with students who brought me books afterward because I had happened to mention I intended to buy them and they wanted to show me they appreciated what I was trying to do for them, they said; visits with authors who had presented me with copies of their own writing; and weeks of planning and going without things on my own part so I could afford to get certain books I felt I must own.

"I wonder whether I'll ever read any of these again?" I asked myself as I packed box after box of books.

On the last day it seemed to me the trees reproached me when I went out to take leave of them. The Chinese elm that had only one green shoot on its spindly, withered trunk that first year now swept over almost the entire roof of the house. The apple and plum trees, lately relieved of their heavy fruit, held their branches high into the air. The evergreens on each side of the opening separating the two parts of the yard had grown so tall and thick that their tops met and formed an arch under which I stood.

"I'll see to it that whoever comes here to live will give you plenty of water," I said, swallowing hard.

Dorothy and I stopped off at Rochester on our way East to make final arrangements for my operation.

While I was sitting in Dr. Benedict's consulting room, I wanted to make him understand that no matter how things turned out with my eyes I would know that the best had been done for them.

"I shall always be grateful to you," I told him. "You have made a new person of me, and the world a wonderful place for me to live in. Ever since you operated on my eyes twenty years ago, I have been able to mingle with people without wondering what they thought of my ugly eyes. No one has had a fuller and happier life than I have since then."

"We could all learn something from you," he said.

"Last time I was here I told you I wasn't a baby," I went on. "But that wasn't true. For weeks after I was at Rochester, I cried day and night. But from now on I'm being a good soldier. I have such faith in you, Dr. Benedict, that if you told me, it would help my eyes to jump into the Atlantic Ocean I'd jump."

Dr. Benedict said he would do all he could to help me so I could see. I should return to Rochester the first part of November. Dorothy insisted that she would accompany me and stay with me while I was at the hospital; but Dr. Benedict dissuaded her, saying it would be unnecessary expense for Dorothy to come with me then.

"Borghild, you have many friends in Rochester who will be glad to do all they can for you," he said, "and if we need Dorothy, we can send for her later."

When we were ready to leave, I told Dr. Benedict I had still one more question to ask him.

"Go ahead and ask," he encouraged me.

'Will it lessen my chances to see if I work on my book?"

'Why, no," he told me. "As long as any light filters into your eye and you can see what you are doing, there is no reason why you shouldn't work as much as you wish."

That was comforting. The time of waiting in New Jersey would pass more quickly if I was busy.

Dorothy had been making her home with the Tottens for several years while teaching in Dover, New Jersey; and so, when I came with her, I stayed there, too.

The finishing of the second draft of the novel I had started during the summer became a kind of race with time for me. All the members of the Totten household tried to help me. Grandma Force and Aunt Alice knew all about life on farms in the seventies and eighties, and since a part of my novel had that for a setting, they contributed many details that I needed to know. Leo was a great lover of horses and could answer any questions I asked him about them. He was painting the woodwork downstairs the first weeks I was at their home, and we talked for hours together. Once he told me a story about his grandparents and I asked his permission to use it.

"Sure," he said, "but that's old stuff and past long ago. Give me an up-to-date prize fight any day."

Estelle was much more emotional, and her advice about developing my characters in situations where they had to be angry or sad or highly excited was often very good. Sometimes when we were working up a scene, we caught ourselves shedding tears, and then we laughed about it afterward.

I was so interested in my work that I grumbled if anything took me away from it while the sun was bright enough so I could make out the typewritten pages which Hazel Thorne faithfully sent me as she finished them. The film on my eye was growing at an alarming speed and I could notice that my working day became considerably shorter with each week. By October I could see only while the sun was at its highest at noon. It was fortunate for me that Dover was having very little cloudy weather.

One day I found myself writing on a page of manuscript which Hazel had already typed. Then I knew it was useless to try to work on my novel anymore.

Time passed more slowly after I couldn't see to write, for there were very few things left for me to do. I spent many hours each day walking. The town was up in the mountains and the streets were, many of them, very steep. However, by being careful I managed.

Koko, Grandma Force's chow, got into the habit of coming with me on my walks. She waited for me in the front hall and if I was late in putting in my appearance, she came upstairs to find me. At first, she wasn't able to resist a spin down a little rabbit path in a wooded lot nearby; but as my sight became poorer, she seemed to sense it, and toward the end she never left my side.

I used to like to walk on the white crushed-rock paths in the Orchard Street cemetery because they were easily seen, and the ground was level. But Koko couldn't come into the cemetery and finally she made such a fuss about my going there without her that I stopped, too.

Koko's affection and protective attitude toward me made me change my mind about the Seeing Eye dogs for the blind. They were trained at Morristown, near Dover, and I often saw them leading their blind masters on the streets. I once used to shudder at the sight of these dogs. Now I began to realize how valuable to a blind person they must be.

I decided that if my operation didn't bring back my sight, I would buy a Seeing Eye dog. I even considered visiting the place where they were trained in order to receive some advance information. But I found I wasn't quite up to this yet.

I needed to be strong for what lay ahead of me, and so I tried out certain kinds of exercises in my room. A cheery voice invited me to join his class in calisthenics which he conducted over the air each morning, and I thought it might be interesting to find out just how much I could get out of his instructions. It would be a new experience to go to school by radio.

The breezy and persistent personality of the teacher soon had me following his instructions as if my very life depended upon his approval. I bent and stretched and lacked and balanced myself while poised on one foot and holding the other in the air. I lay flat on my back and sent my feet so high above my head I was in danger of turning somersaults backwards. I sat on the floor touching my toes with my fingertips and, with my buttocks as a pivot, I swayed my body like the rocker of an old-fashioned cradle. Sometimes I came down on the floor with such a thump that I was worried about the plastering of the ceiling in the dining room below.

The teacher coaxed and sang and chanted and changed our movements. I puffed and panted and sweated with the rest of mv unseen classmates. If for a single moment I tried to take time out to catch my breath, the instructor caught me at it with his seventh radio sense and sent me back into line with my rhythmic bouncing to the time of the music as it came floating over the air.

When at last, completely tired out, I flopped down on the bed and called myself the silliest of sillies for jumping around like a young colt, our teacher would invariably read testimonial letters from grateful followers telling of spectacular changes brought about by his exercises. Immediately I forgot all the names I had called myself and began to think of what we should be doing in the class the next day.

People who had lived in New Jersey all their lives said they had never seen a more perfect September and October. I could feel the warm sunshine and I knew the sky was clear, but I saw less and less of the beauty of the landscape.

When I first came to Dover, the pavement in the country was walled on both sides with masses of green. This green gradually paled into a weak yellow, and some of it warmed up into shades of orange or red or brown. But the walls became narrower, and the coloring faded as if it were being covered with thick layers of dust. Later a few gray trunks standing almost in our path held up bare, gaunt boughs into a gathering mist. Finally, an automobile ride out in the country meant little more to me than the swift passage through a fog that pressed down on me even when I could feel the warmth of the late afternoon sun.

One day I was left alone in the house. Shortly after noon I heard someone on the porch. The rapid opening and closing of the front door and the silence which followed told me that it had been the postman. I went downstairs to find out whether there was any mail for me. By holding the letters up to the window, I could make out my name on one of the envelopes. It was from the college. I tore it open and somehow, I managed to read enough of the letter to know its contents.

My position at the college was no longer open to me.

It was my eyes, they said.

I didn't even try to be brave after I understood this.

I walked from one downstairs room to the other crying hysterically and talking to myself. I couldn't go on living any more. What was the use? People didn't have to go on living when there wasn't anything left to live for. God didn't expect that of anyone.

Oh, those men just didn't realize how much I loved the college and the students and my work or they would never have done this to me. They would have found a way for me to continue lecturing on literature even though I couldn't see. I had committed to memory everything I used in teaching, anyway.

Blind people could teach.

At Concordia College, where Uncle Enoch's children went, there was a blind professor in mathematics. The University of Michigan had kept Dr. Campbell of the chemistry department on for years after he lost his sight—until his death. Paul Mueschke, who

couldn't see at all, was still teaching English there. And if I wasn't mistaken, they had a blind professor at Antioch College, too.

I found myself in the kitchen. I groped my way to the place where I knew the gas stove stood. I fumbled for the handles which turned on the gas. Then I remembered that Estelle had said they had installed an electric range one day while I was gone. I sobbed aloud with disappointment. It would have been so easy to lie down on the floor and never wake up.

I was in the living room again, stumbling against the davenport. I dropped down on it, completely exhausted. For a time, I lay still. My mind was a perfect blank. I didn't try to think any more.

After a little my head began to clear. The feeling of numbness left me.

Then I remembered what I had tried to do, and I cried out in horror. Only cowards gave up like that. What about Helen Keller? In comparison with her handicaps mine was nothing. Yet she didn't admit she was licked.

I began to shed tears again; but this time they were tears of shame instead of self-pity, at the thought of what she had accomplished.

Suppose the one thing that I thought I could do best and that had made me feel useful for so many years had been taken away from me, what then? I was still alive, wasn't I? And wouldn't I find plenty of things that needed to be done if I looked around for them?

In the meantime, I had as big a job as I could handle just now. I would have to exert all the energy I possessed to try to get my sight back. When that had been accomplished, it would be soon enough to think about what I was going to do next.

A story W. L. Murrow told over the Columbia hookup at about this time heartened me greatly.

When the blackouts first came to the larger cities of England, people found it difficult to get around in the dark streets.

One evening a man came up to the radio station in London to tell pedestrians what they should do in order to avoid accidents. He was an expert on traveling in the dark because he had made a study of it for many years. He gave a few simple rules which, if followed, would make walking during blackouts fairly safe. It was better to extend both elbows than the hands in front of one, he said; for the elbows were stronger and closer to the body and could, therefore, brace the body better than the hands in case of a collision with an object.

The man giving the advice to his fellow countrymen on how to avoid accidents on the streets of London was blind. He had lost his sight during the first World War.

I liked this story because it showed me that the Lord always found a place for those who really wanted to work.

On the last Sunday in October there were to be guests to dinner. I dreaded the ordeal. Eating in public was one of the hardest things for me now.

As far back as September the faces of Aunt Alice and Grandma Force, who sat opposite me at the table, had looked to me as though they were under deep water or reflected in a cheap mirror which distorted and dimmed their features^ Gradually I saw less and less of their faces until only what must have been their chins remained. After that there was only a confusion of moving hands and dishes and indistinguishable food against the white cloth on their side of the table, and their voices were all that told me that they were there. Leo at my left and Dorothy and Estelle at my right stayed with me longer. But soon they, too, became shadowy forms with nothing but their voices to let me know for sure that they were in their places.

On Sunday when the guests came to dinner, we all sat down together at the table. While Leo served, Dorothy, as she always did now, told me quietly what we were having to eat and where my servings were placed on the table near me. I was going to pick up my fork when I realized that, instead, I had dipped the fingers of my left hand into something wet and mushy. I pulled my hand back at once.

"Never mind," Dorothy whispered. "It's only your applesauce. Here, wipe your hand on your napkin."

I heard Estelle get up and come around to my chair.

"Here is another napkin," she said, also so low that only I could hear her.

I was so upset, however, that my dinner was spoiled.

"Only your applesauce."

"When you find that your vision is entirely gone, come back to us and we'll see what we can do for you."

I knew that the time that Dr. Benedict meant when he said this had come.

I was blind.

It was terrible to wake up every morning to find that it was as dark as it had been the night before. Actually, I had been seeing almost nothing for weeks, but the realization that I was blind now had such a finality about it that it frightened me.

I kept thinking of gay flames dancing in cozy fireplaces, beautiful rooms all ablaze with lights, wide stretches of water where the moon was reflected in streaks of shining silver, and the dazzling sunshine.

How could anyone grumble who was allowed to enjoy such miracles day and night?

If ever I regained my sight, I told myself, I would never stop looking at these things.

Hearing that I was soon to leave for Rochester, friends of Dorothy and the Tottens dropped in to wish me good luck and they brought me presents of perfume, candy, and silk underwear. They told me the underwear was blue and pink and peach-colored, and I enjoyed touching it with my fingers and appreciated the kindness that went with the gifts.

As I sat by myself in the dark, I prayed. I prayed that things wouldn't turn out too bad with me and that I would have courage enough to take them if they did. Sometimes I could only think of God and feel a prayer inside of me without saying it in words.

This continuous praying seemed to calm me, and toward the end of the week I became more cheerful. The night before I left for Rochester I slept as quietly and peacefully as a baby.

Saturday morning, Dorothy packed the last things that were going into my bags and closed them while I was dressing. I could hear Koko's footfalls following me and I had to be careful not to stumble over her. Leo came home from work at about ten and did all sorts of little kindnesses for me. We had lunch an hour early and everyone pretended that that was why none of us could eat anything. At the last-minute Dorothy emptied her new purse and transferred the contents of mine into it, saying hers was roomier than mine.

The wind was cool and blew against our faces as we drove to the depot, but there was no longer the depressing rain that had been coming down all week. The station master came out and told us where to stand, since my train was an express and was making a special stop for me. We heard its whistle in the distance, and a minute later it was thundering into the station.

Dorothy and the Tottens scarcely had time to kiss me good-by before the conductor and the brakeman stepped down on the platform and helped me into the train. As soon as I had reached my seat, I felt the movement of the train and knew I was on my way.

The porter took my wraps, brought me a pillow, and helped me touch a button with my hand so I could push it whenever I needed anything.

It must have been toward evening when the dining car conductor brought me the menu and read it aloud to me. He asked me whether I preferred to have my dinner served to me in the Pullman or if I would like to come with him into the diner. I chose the latter. I would be less conspicuous, I thought, and it would rest me to walk a little.

I decided to go to bed early. The day had seemed very long. The porter brought me to the ladies' room and then helped me into my berth. I undressed in my berth so I wouldn't lose my clothes carrying them around. From force of habit, I still wore my glasses, and I put them carefully into the case I kept in my purse. I tied both my stockings together in a knot and stuffed them into one of my shoes. And I put this shoe into the empty one and fastened the two of them and my purse with a ribbon inside the little hammock that hung close to the window. I was careful that these were at the same end of the berth as my head.

"I'll hang your dress on a hanger," the porter said.

I handed it to him through the opening that I found in the heavy curtains by fumbling around a little.

"I gave you an extra blanket," the porter told me. "I was afraid you might take a chill. The nights up in the mountains are pretty cold now."

I couldn't sleep, but I didn't mind. I felt closer to God than I had ever been in my life, and I prayed all night. It seemed to me that if He only knew how much I wanted to see He would think of a way to help me. I kept begging Him to let me see, and after a while I noticed that I was praying in time with the clicking of the wheels against the railway ties:

Please, oh, please; oh, please, O Lord, Please let me see; please let me see.

Please, oh, please; oh, please, O Lord, Please let me see; please let me see.

Please, oh, please; oh, please, O Lord, Please let me see; please let me see.

I repeated this prayer almost without stopping until it was morning.

The porter returned my dress and later brought me into the diner for breakfast. After the train had begun to slow down in the outskirts of Chicago, he put all my baggage into the seat beside me and helped me on with my wraps.

"Don't have a care in the world," he told me. "Everything it tended to. Just take it easy and you're going to be all right."

His rich Southern accent was as soothing as his reassuring words, and when the train pulled into the station I wasn't at all frightened.

"Are you Miss Dahl?" someone asked pleasantly as the porter helped me to the platform. "I am the chief of the La Salle Street Station. I am here to see that you are taken over to the other depot."

He took my arm and piloted me through the crowd that buzzed around us.

"We had wires last night that you were aboard this train," he told me. "One from Buffalo and another from Cleveland."

I heard him greet people, and all the time he kept up a cheerful conversation with me.

"Were in the La Salle Street Station now. I'm taking you over to the Parmelee bus."

The ride from one depot to the other was short. In only a few minutes I was being delivered to someone in the Union Station.

"I'm sorry you're having trouble with your eyes," this man said as we walked through the station. "I hear you're being sent to Rochester to the Mayos. I hope they're going to be able to help you."

I realized that I was being ushered to a seat.

"I'll have to ask you to sit down here for a little," the man said. "Your train isn't quite ready yet. Just rest and don't worry. I'll be back soon."

I traveled in a day coach during the remainder of the trip. It was more tiring, but I rather enjoyed the change. There was a constant bustle about me. Passengers entered and left the coach at every station. In the afternoon I began to hear the familiar names of Wisconsin towns: Madison, Sparta, West Salem. Then I smelled a freshwater breeze coming in through the window and I guessed we must have reached the Mississippi. The hollow echo I heard immediately afterward told me we were on a railway bridge and were approaching the Minnesota side of the river.

The conductor walked through the train and called off a stop for lunch at Winona. I thought I was too tired to eat; but a girl came over to me and offered to bring me a sandwich and a cup of coffee, and I accepted her kindness with thanks. After this introduction the girl and I visited together, and the time passed more quickly.

"Rochester, Rochester, Rochester. This way out," the conductor called.

I had arrived at my destination.

I was paged as soon as the train stopped. A man led me across the platform at the Rochester station and put me into a waiting automobile.

"Where do you want to go?" he asked me.

"Where? Don't you know?" I exclaimed, much surprised. "Aren't you from the Mayo Clinic?"

"I'm a representative of the Northwestern Railroad," the man said. "I was notified from New York to meet you here tonight and to see that you were taken where you wanted to go."

I was so nervous that I felt myself shaking all over.

"I thought you were from the clinic," I repeated. "I really don't know where I'm supposed to go. Someone from the clinic was to meet me, I thought."

"You're in a taxi now," the man from the Northwestern Railroad told me.

I tried to think quickly. I was sure Dorothy had told me that someone from the clinic would meet me, and that I was going to be taken directly to a hospital. But which one? For my other operation I was at the Worrall. But that was twenty years ago, and much had changed around Rochester since then. Well, it would be best to try the Worrall first. So, I told the man from the Northwestern Railroad that I would manage and asked the taxi driver to take me to the Worrall Hospital.

When I arrived in the lobby of the hospital, the young man at the desk said that no reservations had been made for me. My heart

almost stopped beating. There had been something uncanny about being handed from one stranger to the other without being able to see any of them, and now when I suddenly found myself alone with someone who had never heard of me, I was in a panic.

"I'm in a hospital, am I not?" I asked, trying to conceal from the young man how frightened I was.

"Yes, you're at the Worrall," he answered courteously. "Does Dr. Benedict still do his operating here?" I asked.

"Yes, he does."

"I'm his patient. I just arrived on the train from New Jersey. I'm supposed to have an operation tomorrow."

I wondered what it would be best for me to do.

"Do you have a room where I might stay tonight?" I asked.

Yes, that could be arranged, he said. But before I could be shown to one, I would have to make a deposit of fifty dollars.

This announcement floored me. I didn't have that much money in cash with me. And, even if I had, I couldn't see to count it out in paper bills. Dorothy had supplied me with silver change which I could distinguish by feeling of it But fifty dollars! I had my checkbook somewhere in my purse, but I hadn't thought of that since leaving Dover because I didn't expect to use it until later. Anna Seem would be coming in the morning and she would look after such matters for me. I asked whether I couldn't wait until then, but it seemed this wasn't possible.

In my confusion I couldn't find my checkbook. The young man at the desk offered to fill out a blank check for me, but I said I wanted to use one from my own bank in New Jersey.

"If you could show me my room," I said at last, "I'm sure I could find my check blanks. Then if you'll make out my check for me, I'll sign it."

For the life of me I couldn't keep a catch out of my voice.

I smelled antiseptics when I walked through the corridor toward my room. This was reassuring to me because I could at least be positive of being in a hospital. In my own room I emptied the contents of my purse out on the bed and found the missing checkbook. The young man was waiting outside my door, and he brought me farther down the corridor to a

 desk. Here he made out a check for me and directed my hand to the place where I was to sign it.

"I should like to send a telegram and put in a long-distance telephone call" I said after the matter of the fifty-dollar deposit had been attended to.

The young man said both could be taken care of right at the desk where we were.

I dictated the telegram to Dorothy: "Had a good trip. Am in fine spirits. Love. Borghild."

I had no trouble in making my telephone connection to Harmony. It was good to hear Anna Seem's voice. She told me she would be at the hospital early in the morning.

Anna's manner was cheerful and matter of fact. Since she was with me during my last operation, it gave me a feeling of confidence to see her now.

The nurse came to tell me that Dr. Benedict had arrived at the hospital. He would come to me after he had made the rounds of his other patients.

"You're not able to see at all now," Dr. Benedict said after he had examined my eye.

"I walked downtown the day before I left New Jersey," I told him. It was the*truth, too. I went to the beauty parlor to have a manicure and my hair done. Leo watched for me at his filling station and helped me across Blackwell Street.

Dr. Benedict said the ambulance had been at the station to meet me the night before, but the men in charge of it hadn't been able to find me. The man from the Northwestern Railroad must have brought me into the taxi before the ambulance attendants could page me. I realized how stupid I had been not to have sent the man from the Northwestern Railroad in search of the people from the clinic.

"How would you like to have that cataract out this afternoon?" Dr. Benedict asked me.

I said that would be all right for me.

"Is there anything more that I can do but hope and pray, Dr. Benedict?" I asked him as he was leaving.

"No, I guess you have everything else that it takes," he answered gently.

All forenoon the nurses were busy getting me ready for the operation. Anna came and went. She took down the names of relatives and close friends who were to be notified about how things went with me. She unpacked my bags and laid the clothes I

would be needing at the hospital into the dresser drawers. She read passages out of the Bible to me. And we prayed. There was the same peace and trust in God in my heart now that I had felt during the night on the train.

The rattle of dishes out in the hall told me that lunch was being served to the other patients.

Anna closed the door.

I fell on my knees beside my bed.

"Dear God," I prayed, "be with me today. Direct the hand and the brain of him whom Thou hast sent to help me. I want so very much to see. But, if this can't be, please give me courage so I can go on living anyway."

Then Anna and I repeated the Lord's Prayer together.

After that the nurse came for me. She said Anna might come, too. I was taken farther down the hall and into a very narrow room, where I was told to lie down on a couch. The nurse gave me a capsule which she said would make me sleep. Then she left the room.

But I couldn't sleep. Anna and I prayed.

There was a slight noise at the door. I heard a man's voice.

It was Dr. Quill, the house doctor.

"We are ready for you now," he said quietly.

I took a quick breath and raised myself on the couch.

Anna kissed me.

The house doctor led me into the operating room.

This time Anna didn't come with me.

After I had lain down on the operating table, someone in the room began to sing. Although I thought I was calm, the singing bothered me.

"I don't like that music," I said irritably.

"A person has to use the voice that was given to him," someone near me said.

"Dear me," I thought, "I mustn't start out like this."

I could hear the rustle of skirts around me, and the soft footsteps of people walking about the room. A faucet was turned on and there was a sound of trickling water.

"There isn't anything wrong with your voice," I apologized. "It's only that I'm a little nervous just now."

"I thought we had given you something to take the edge off things," the same voice said, but this time it was kind and sympathetic.

"What kind of anesthetic are you giving me?" I asked a nurse at my side.

"Local. Cocaine," she said.

So, I was going to be awake all the time and know what they were doing to me. I hadn't expected that.

"Don't try to do anything for yourself while you're lying here," the nurse said. "If your face itches or you're uncomfortable in any other way, let us know. We'll do everything for you."

There was more and more activity around me. Someone scrubbed my face and washed it with a disinfectant. Then drops were put into my eyes—at first into only the one that was going to be operated on and later into the socket of the other one, too. There was also a needle injection into my face near the left ear. Each time something was done, the doctors and nurses had told me about it beforehand; so, I wasn't startled or frightened.

"Dr. Benedict is in the room now," the house doctor said to me.

There was a long silence. Then a slight stirring near me.

"Dr. Benedict is with you now," the house doctor said. "You can help him a great deal by doing exactly what he tells you to do."

There was more stirring around me. This time closer than before. Otherwise, there was a dead silence in the room.

I could hear the breathing of someone very close to me.

"Never look up. Nor in. No matter what happens. Always down. And to the left. Not quite so much. That's better."

It was Dr. Benedict's voice I heard now.

I could feel that he was beginning to work on my eye. There was only a slight touch of something that came in contact with it. I held my breath. Not a muscle must move. Not a twitch.

Steady. Steady. Steady.

Then all at once, high above me, a ball of fire appeared out of the dark. And a curved luminous thread, like the wire in a lighted electric bulb.

"Irrigate."

Again, it was Dr. Benedict's voice.

Then everything about me went black once more.

I felt myself being lifted and carried somewhere.

"Don't drop me," I heard myself say. "I'm heavy."

"You needn't worry about that. There are five people holding you. Besides, we have brought much bigger women than you out of this room."

It was Dr. Benedict who spoke to me this time, too.

I was back in my bed. Someone was putting bands on my wrists.

"We are tying your hands," a nurse told me, "so you won't touch your eye and hurt it."

Then I thought I could feel that Dr. Benedict was in the room. He was talking to me. I recognized his voice. He was really there then. Oh, God, I must ask him.

But my own voice. What had happened to it? I strained myself so I shivered from the exertion.

"Dr. Benedict, am I going to see?"

At last, the question was out. I died and came to life again a hundred times while I waited for his answer.

"Who said you aren't going to see?"

Chapter 10

"Thank you, God."

I felt the words inside of me.

Dr. Benedict spoke to me again.

"You will try to lie perfectly quiet, won't you? Without moving except just enough to prevent your neck from becoming stiff."

Out of the darkness I could hear his voice. He told me he would wire Dorothy.

"She will believe you," I heard myself saying.

Anna came for only a minute. She said she would write to Uncle Enoch and Aunt Elizabeth and to my sisters.

It was queer how tired I was all at once. Even sipping water out of a straw was a tremendous chore. People were walking on tiptoe. Someone said my sisters from Minneapolis had come. Esther and Ellen. I recognized them when they said my name.

"We're only going to stay for a minute. Selmer is waiting for us downstairs."

One of my sisters held my hand. I couldn't move it because it was tied. A kiss was pressed upon it and drops of something fell on it—tears.

Then only silence and darkness once more.

It must have been during the night that I became frightened. I didn't know why. Anna was there. She held my hand, and then I couldn't remember anything more.

The pain woke me up. More capsules and more water held to my lips to be sipped through a straw. Darkness and forgetfulness. But after that the racket with the eye started all over again, and then there was the round of capsules and water out of a straw and the blackness once more. It was a kind of marathon of pain followed by forgetfulness. But the pain had all the odds on its side.

Dr. Quill, the house doctor who had helped Dr. Benedict in the operating room, came to see me. He was a fine fellow after I got to know him. I began to look forward to his visits.

Many nurses were in and out of the room. At first, I knew only in a confused sort of way that they were there. But out of the blackness their footsteps, their voices, the touch of their hands, and something else about them helped me to tell which was which. Soon I was able to call them by name: Miss Heller, Miss Schenk, Miss Rose, Miss Anderson, Miss Taft. They were kind and efficient. Just when I was sure my back had been broken in two, it was made to feel whole again by firm, gentle hands that rubbed it in the place where it hurt the most. Those hands also placed pillows in the hollows of the bed where it didn't fit the bulges of my body and washed soothing lotions over chafed elbows and heels that had braced themselves too hard to help the eye endure its pain.

The day came when the bandages were to be taken off for the first time. Dr. Quill was in the room. The nurses raised the headrest of the bed. I sat holding my breath.

The tips of Dr. Quill's fingers touched my cheek as they unfastened the bandage. I could feel that it no longer covered my eye.

But everything was dark. I had to lie back on my pillow. Oh, God, I couldn't see after all.

Dr. Quill put drops into the eye, and the bandage back on my face. I couldn't let him go away without asking him.

"Is my eye all right?"

"Why, yes."

But he hesitated as he spoke, and I thought I detected doubt in his manner.

A little later Dr. Benedict came in to see me.

"Dr. Quill has already dressed my eye," I told him excitedly. "If it isn't all right, won't you please come back and tell me?"

"Don't worry. I'll come back," he promised.

He did, too, bringing Dr. Quill with him. Dr. Benedict himself removed the bandage this time, and he explained to Dr. Quill that there was a little glaucoma in the eye. Then Dr. Benedict comforted me by saying that the condition of my eye was as satisfactory as could be expected so soon after the operation.

But, after that, every time Dr. Quill took off the bandage, I could scarcely wait to find out whether I could see. And when I discovered I was still in the dark, I had all I could do to keep myself from crying out with disappointment.

I began to worry for fear I should never be able to see any more. Perhaps some new complication had set in. I remembered that Dr. Benedict had once told Dr. Prangen that my eye had had just about everything that could happen to it, and yet that was before this last trouble.

Maybe this cheerfulness around me was put on, I told myself. Maybe people at the hospital were keeping the truth away from me until they thought I was strong enough to hear it.

I kept thinking I heard Dorothy's voice in the corridor; if this were true, things were in a bad way with me. I repeated to myself what Dr. Benedict had said when Dorothy and I stopped off at Rochester on our way East.

"If we need Dorothy, we can send for her later."

The black nights seemed endless. But always Dr. Benedict's cheery "Good morning" reassured me, and his optimism and kindly humor gave me hope that I would eventually come out of the dark. At last, one morning after Dr. Quill had removed the bandage, the ebony screen which had shut me out from the rest of the world had changed to a dull gray. It reminded me of the dripping, autumn fog in a seaport town.

"We can see a little today," Dr. Quill exclaimed. "Now let's have a try at how well we can do it. Can you tell me how many fingers I am holding up?"

I guessed at the answer, but the fact that I could make out anything at all was proof that I could see.

The tears trickled down my cheeks and I didn't care who saw them.

I began to see a little more each time the eye was uncovered. I knew the nurses at my bedside wore white uniforms, and soon I could make out blurred suggestions of their faces.

"What can we see today?" Dr. Quill asked one morning after the eye had been responding to light for several days.

"A handsome Lochinvar," I answered, laughing.

"Then I'm awfully sorry to have to tell you that you're not seeing at all as you should," he said, pretending to be disappointed.

I was really in dead earnest about the compliment I had paid him. Dr. Quill's were the first features I had seen at all clearly in months, and right then, to me, he was the handsomest man in the world.

At last, the bandages were left off entirely and a pair of smoked glasses were brought down for me from the storeroom upstairs. After I got so, I could wear them comfortably, I knew I was going to be able to get along by myself and walk around out of doors without the aid of a Seeing Eye dog. When I realized this fully, I was so thrilled that I decided to call Dorothy in New Jersey and tell her the wonderful news.

There was a long delay getting Dover, and when the operator finally told me that my party was on the line, I could only hold the receiver and stutter.

"I-I-I can see, Dorothy," I repeated over and over again. "I-I can see. I can see."

It was wonderful to lie and watch the daylight come out of the blackness around me every morning. I couldn't keep from looking toward the east; and yet at the first appearance of the sun above the skyline, I had to bury my face in the pillow because I couldn't stand the pain from its dazzling brightness.

I was almost as excited at the prospect of going to the clinic to have my eye tested for glasses as I had been over the removal of the bandages.

However, when I arrived there, I learned that Dr. Prangen was out of the city. I was so disappointed that I almost told the nurse that I would wait until his return, but I decided that this would be silly. So, I went with her into the room where the new doctor was to examine my eye. I had never been there before, and I was nervous from the start.

The doctor handed me a card just as Dr. Prangen used to do. I had begun to bring it close to my face, as I always had, when the doctor spoke to me rather sharply.

"Don't do that," he said. "You are all over that myopia now. Hold the card at a distance from your eyes."

I did as he told me, but I couldn't make out a single word.

"You'll probably have some difficulty gauging your distances at first" he said. "Keep trying until you can read what is on the card."

I brought the card back to my face once more and gradually drew it away, but this didn't do any good. The doctor came over and tried to help me, but I couldn't read even the largest print. He had me turn to the chart on the wall, but this was even worse.

I was so disappointed that I had all I could do to keep the tears back.

"Can't you find a glass that will fit my eye?" I begged the doctor. "I want to see so badly."

The doctor tried again, but none of the lenses he held up to my eye helped me.

"Perhaps we aren't going to be able to fit you with glasses," Dr. Benedict said after he had heard the results of the tests. "Your eye turns up and in and that complicates matters for you in the fitting of the glasses. However, we have always been able to find a suitable lens in the past for you; and it may be that if we wait, we can do better later."

It was almost a month after this when I returned to the clinic at Rochester once more. To my great relief Dr. Pran-gen was back. He didn't mind how close I held the card, but I could tell for myself that the letters looked clearer farther away from my face. By working over the words, I succeeded in reading the coarsest print with the first lens he held up to my eye, but after he had tried a few others, I did it more easily. Just turning a lens upside down or inside out often made a perceptible difference in my ability to see through it. I kept trying distances for the card, but it was hard to see which was best.

Finally, Dr. Prangen put a lens into a frame and, slipping its bows behind my ears, told me to read aloud to him what I could see on the card. I kept right on until I had reached the end of the coarsest print.

He seemed satisfied, for I could hear him chuckling softly.

I was jubilant.

"I don't have to ask you what you want for Christmas this year," Dr. Prangen said, taking off the frames. "I see you have your gift already."

The glasses were sent to me by mail from Rochester to Harmony, where I was staying with Anna Seem and her mother. The glasses arrived after dark. The next morning, I put on those for distance vision and walked over to the front window. Ever since my arrival from the hospital I had been looking out there, and all I had been able to see was a grayish-brown mass. Now there was stubble in a field that was left from the last harvest and, farther away, a large woods. I could make out separate trees in the woods, each of which had many branches. Those that caught the rays of the sun were lighter and warmer in color than the rest.

"This is a wonderful day," I told Mrs. Seem. "I'm so happy that I have to do something. If your feet didn't hurt you so much, I'd simply make you come along with me. As it is, I'll have to celebrate alone."

I wore my red dress because it was the gayest one, I owned. Then I put on my wraps.

"I can't stay inside. The house isn't big enough for me today."

I walked down in the business section of Main Street. I looked at the shopwindows. I was amazed at the fine assortments of goods the merchants had on display. The buildings themselves were exciting, too, for I could see every brick and board they were made of. The whole landscape seemed as bright and clean as if it had been treated to a good scrubbing.

I returned to the Seems' for lunch as I had promised Mrs. Seem I would. We two were alone. I played with each bean, balancing it on my fork; and I picked up only one round cherry at a time in my spoon, watching the dish as it was gradually being emptied.

"You aren't eating at all today," Mrs. Seem told me. "I guess you are too excited."

"Yes, I'm too happy to eat today," I told her.

I went visiting all afternoon. First to Emma Rostvold's. She was with me when Dr. Prangen found the correct lens for me, and so she knew how much the day meant to me. But I didn't stay there long. I had to hurry on. I stopped but a few minutes at each place. To those I visited I must have appeared like a child rushing in to show them a new Christmas toy. Yet I had nothing new. Even the frames of my glasses were old.

I was doing the seeing today. I was pointing out to others what there was to be seen. Others would soon be singing, "Silent night, holy night." I wanted to shout so everyone could hear me: "All is bright. Joy to the world."

At last, I was too tired to go any farther. I returned to the Seems', but on my way back I took a different route. I wouldn't miss any opportunity to see all I could.

It was late when I reached the house. Anna was already there, and I saw tears in her eyes.

My eye had reacted well to the distance lens, but with the one for close work it was different. It was difficult to see through a high plus lens after having required a high minus one all my life. The muscles of my eye, too, had grown weak because I hadn't used it for a long time, and I had to train it just as an athlete exercises certain parts of his body when he is getting ready for a contest in some special kind of sport.

First of all, I had to find print that was of a size that I could read comfortably, and then I had to learn to use my eye the new way.

To begin with I could just manage to spell out the largest headlines in the newspapers, and even these weren't clear until I had looked at them for a while. For days I worked over them and looked hungrily at the smaller headlines and the long columns of the regular print without being able to read a single word.

Then I began to make out a word here and there in the smaller type of the headlines and I wondered whether there wouldn't be some book that had print large enough for me to manage. I found my level in Mother Goose. At once I went about reading the short rhymes in this as though my life depended upon it. In the first one I stumbled over the words that told the story of Bobby Shafto. It took a long time to read it; and when I had finished, my eye was red and ached. But I kept right on, and the second story, Betty Two Shoes, required only half the time and my eye wasn't nearly as tired afterward. Pretty soon I could read Mother Goose almost as quickly and as easily as I had read regular print before I got the cataract.

Then I looked about for something a little harder. I found a child's primer in the bookcase, and I decided to try that. I turned to the first page, on which was a highly colored picture of a boy, two little girls, and a dog. All three stood beside a fence. This seemed promising. I began to read.

SEE IT GO

"Look," said Dick.

"See it go.

"See it go up."

That wasn't so bad. I turned to the next page.

Jane said, "Oh, look!

"See it go.

"See it go up." . . . "Up, up," said Sally, "Go up, up, up."

It gave me immense satisfaction to have finished these two pages. The print was smaller than that in Mother Goose, and I had read it almost as well. Anna brought me other books from the juvenile section of the library, and I read them.

One day she showed me a book she had picked up from the shelf for older boys and girls. It was Richard Halliburton's Book of Marvels. The print, although not quite as good as in the others, was very clear and I found I could read it, and I enjoyed it especially because of the information contained in it. Now reading had become something more than the mere practice of deciphering letters and words.

"Perhaps you are ready for still finer print," Anna suggested.

But the smaller type looked blurred, and so I had to go back to books with larger print. I read these each day as long as I could without straining my eye. It grew stronger and eventually I could keep on for hours without tiring it at all. Then I tried the finer print once more. Now I was able to read it, but I found that I had to return to my old schedule of only a sentence or two at a sitting.

Sometimes I grew impatient at the slow progress I was making.

"What do you expect?" Mrs. Seem scolded. "You have been out of the hospital less than three months."

"Yes, but I can't read children's books all my life," I grumbled.

"If you didn't read a single book for a year," she said, "you would still have read more than your share. How many people, even with good eyes, do you think have been able to carry on the way you have been doing all your life?"

Mrs. Seems rather severe manner made me stop and think Maybe I had expected too much. There was such a thing as tempting providence. I told myself. Yet I knew that I just wouldn't be able to keep myself from going the limit until I had pulled myself out of the helpless state into which I had so suddenly been plunged.

I saw Dr. Benedict again in March. He examined my eye carefully, but he made no comment afterward. Neither did he send me into Dr. Prangen's office to have my eye tested for permanent glasses as I had been sure he would. Was his manner slightly strained or was it only my overly active imagination at work again, I asked myself. I wondered whether it could be that he wasn't pleased with the progress of my eye.

"Is anything wrong?" I asked, my heart beginning to beat so hard that I could hear it under the blue knit dress I was wearing.

"No," he replied.

But I wasn't satisfied. However, Dr. Benedict had nothing more to say about the eye, although he continued to look grave.

"Did you come alone?" he asked after a little.

"Of course. Why shouldn't I?"

"Can you read now?"

"Yes," I answered promptly, neglecting, however, to mention the pain I often felt of late while I was doing it.

"And your handwriting?" he persisted.

"Sure. Can you?"

He laughed outright at this question. Everyone familiar with my script would understand the reason.

"Yes, I can," he said.

Then he told me to return to the clinic in May.

I lay awake nights worrying about this visit with Dr. Benedict. Was something terrible going to happen to my eye again? His manner was certainly strange and, worst of all, I was pretty sure that I noticed I was seeing less than I had been doing.

In May, after an examination in the darkroom, Dr. Benedict told me that my eye was misbehaving again. There was another film growing over it—a secondary cataract, he called it. This wasn't nearly as bad as the first one and was common in ordinary cases of cataract. With my eye it was rather to have been expected, since the first operation, out of necessity, had had to be of a conservative nature. The film would, of course, have to be removed.

"That would have to happen to me," I said, almost in tears.

"Oh, but the worst is over," Dr. Benedict consoled me. "Think what this second operation will mean to you. Since you can read as well as you are doing with your eye as it is now, you will eventually be able to read any kind of print. That is, if all goes well; and this time the risk isn't nearly as great as it was before."

The curtain over my eye grew heavier every day. Again, I began to have to be careful of my footing. I had more and more trouble in seeing to read. Only the tops of the letters showed on the printed page and gradually these began to disappear, too. It was as though wads of cotton were being placed at random all over the page. At last, every word I read meant a struggle, and finally I gave up trying entirely.

The strain of not being able to see affected my nerves. I became extremely sensitive to noise, and I was depressed most of the time. It had been such fun being able to see, and this dimming of my vision again, temporary as Dr. Benedict promised it would be, frightened me. The worry over the risk I had to take every time anything was done to my eye was telling on me.

Apparently, I was sane on every subject in the world except one. That was my eyes. If anything concerned them, I was a hopeless alarmist.

It was like coming home to arrive at the Worrall Hospital again. There was no doubt about my belonging there this time. The young man at the desk recognized me. Mrs. Whiting and Mrs. Donahue, the supervisors on fourth floor, received me with open arms. Everything about the place was cozily familiar.

The nurse in the operating room treated me as though I was a veteran at the game. After I had stretched out on the table, she let me tuck myself into the operating robe.

I wasn't nervous at all. It was like getting my old job back to relax on the operating table and to turn my thumbs under my body to prevent my hands from becoming numb.

As I lay there waiting for the operation to commence, I thought I felt a hairpin prodding into my head. It didn't exactly hurt me, but it was annoying. I made a sudden move to raise myself into a sitting position when I realized that everything was set to begin working on me.

"Whew!" someone exclaimed; in fact, several people said it at once.

"I was just going to fix my hairpin," I said. "It's sticking me.

"You can stand it a little, can't you?"

It was Dr. Benedict who asked me this question "Sure, I can."

I lay back on the table once more.

But I was thrilled at what I had seen. A tall white figure from whose snowy helmet blazed a dazzling light like the pictures of the flaming torch of wisdom. It was as though I had caught a glimpse of Balder, the god of light and sunshine, from whom, according to the old Norse legend, radiated love and light that cheered mortals in the darkness of the Arctic circle.

The operation took only a few minutes. Just a testing at first to determine whether there was any pain in the eye at its contact with the surgical instruments. A stroke of Dr. Benedict's hand. Irrigation. The bandage. Total darkness once more. And that was all.

"That's the last operation I'm performing on you, lady," Dr. Benedict promised me as I was being lifted to the cart.

I was wheeled back to my room, and the operation about which I had done so much fretting and worrying was over.

The next day when I was released from the hospital, I learned it had been entirely successful.

Chapter 11

I was no longer blind.

To be exact, I could see forty times as well as I had at my other time in my life.

In addition to the two kinds of glasses which Dr. Granger had prescribed for me—those for distance seeing and the ones for close work—I had, at Dr. Benedict's suggestion, supplied myself with several reading glasses to be used on special occasions. The largest one covered the entire page of a book when I held it properly and this enabled me to read much faster and lessened the strain on my eye. Another was smaller and could be used to read passages of especially fine print. The smallest and strongest glass was helpful in reading maps, graphs, timetables, and such things.

And now it was time for me to think seriously about what I was going to do with all this sight that had been given me. How could I again make myself useful in the world? By what means could I earn my living once more?

There was no doubt in my mind as to what I should like best to do. I wanted to go right on with my writing and make a career of it. But the question to be considered was: did I have enough talent for this? And did I really, now that the test was at hand, have anything to say that would be of actual benefit to people?

Well, there was only one way to find out. That was to try.

After I had been able to see well enough and was strong enough to work, I had gone back to my novel that I had been working on in New Jersey. I had had it typed in June and after Anna and Mrs. Seem and I had each given it an encouraging tap and had drunk a toast to its success, I had sent it off to its first publisher. It had come back from that one and from several others. But I hadn't been discouraged because two of the publishers had taken the trouble to write me friendly letters with their rejection slips and I had felt sure that they had liked something about the book.

While in Minneapolis visiting with my sister Esther, I had tried my hand at short stories. But I had all the time been rather at sea and I had felt that if I could only receive some expert direction in my writing I would know better where I was at.

"Why don't you ask Marchette Chute to look over something you have written?" a friend asked me one day. "She's a wonderful critic."

I begged my friend to tell me about this critic. Did my friend think she would care to bother with me, a mere beginner?

"It wouldn't hurt to ask her," my friend said enthusiastically. "It isn't only Marchette Chute's literary opinion that would help you. She has such a sympathetic attitude toward life that she would bring out the best in you as no ordinary critic could do."

I succeeded in getting in contact with Marchette Chute and she consented to look over two of my short stories. I wasn't very proud of them because I knew I hadn't spent enough time on them, but they would at least be a start. Besides, she could get some idea from them, bad as they were, of how I wrote.

A young woman in tweeds greeted me in the parlor at the Y.W.C.A., where I had an appointment to meet my new critic. She was slight and dark and to me she was lovely.

"I am Marchette Chute," she told me in a low, musical voice, "and I believe you are Miss Dahl."

After we were seated on a davenport, she began to tell me what she thought of my two stories. I knew she wasn't especially impressed with them, but at once her kind frankness gave me confidence in her.

Before I realized what was happening, I was pouring out to her my story. I told her about my blindness and the effect it had had on my life. She was a stranger to me and yet I revealed to her feelings that lay deep down in my heart-something I had never been guilty of doing before. I, who shrank from mentioning my eyes to my immediate family and to lifelong friends.

We talked all morning. I rose to go.

But Marchette Chute detained me.

"Why don't you write your own story?" she asked me.

I felt self-conscious at once. It had been foolish of me to talk openly as I had.

"Oh, no," I said. "I'm sorry I bothered you. People don't care to hear about the troubles of others. They don't want to listen to whiners."

She smiled encouragingly.

"But that's exactly what you are not. That is why I suggested that you write about yourself."

I stood thinking. Far back in my memory came the picture of my gray-haired teacher. Miss Cox. The one who reminded me of Queen Victoria and who, the day I was absent from school, told the rest of the children in my room how proud she was of me because I tried so hard to overcome the handicap of my eyes.

"All of us have handicaps," Maria Sanford at the University of Minnesota told me when I started out to teach.

"Think of the good you could do if you told your story," Marchettc Chute was saying. "People with handicaps would take courage by your example and think, 'Miss Dahl got along with those eyes of hers. I guess I can with my troubles, too, if I tackle the job as she did.' "

Still, I hesitated.

"You would be helping others, too. Your story would convince them that a person with even a serious handicap can be both useful and extremely happy, and that the greatest kindness anyone can show such a person is to treat him exactly like anyone else."

"I'll do it," I said at last, taking Marchette Chute's hand, "and now I know what will keep me busy up at Uncle Enoch's and Aunt Elizabeth's home in Twin Valley this winter."

We talked a little more about the book.

"Will you be willing to help me with it and criticize it for me as I go along?" I asked.

"I'll be glad to," Marchette Chute said. "I'm going to California, but you can easily send me your chapters through the mail."

I went away feeling grateful and happier than I had been in months. I had my work to do now.

I had come expecting to meet a critic. I had found a real friend.

Now I am again living in Twin Valley with Uncle Enoch and Aunt Elizabeth, and we are back to where we were twenty-eight years ago. Then I was starting out on a new career just as I am doing now.

Uncle Enoch and Aunt Elizabeth are encouraging me now to think that I can accomplish what I set out to do just as they did then. Aunt Elizabeth, especially, has the most comfortable way of making me believe that I am something, even though, deep down in my heart, I suspect differently. But the surprising thing is that she is so clever at deceiving me that I have become almost what she pretended I. was.

Now she nets as though my ambition to v/rite is the most natural thing in the world. After I have read aloud to her a chapter of my story, she tells me it is wonderful. Her praise, undeserved though

it may be, gives me confidence to go on and I am beginning to think I can do things once more.

I am washing dishes at the kitchen sink. Through the window I can see a flock of sparrows flying into the birdhouse set upon a pole in the back yard. I have never been able to see this birdhouse clearly until this winter. Now I know it is painted a bright green and has many doors in it. Aunt Elizabeth says it has room for sixteen bird families. I can see the dapping of the gray-black wings of the sparrows as they fly through the thick, falling snow.

I return to my dishwashing, which, because of my interest in the birds, I have completely forgotten.

Uncle Enoch enters the room, and I turn to hear what he is saying. I know he has been watching me while I have been enjoying the birds. His eyes are beaming with the same kind of encouragement and love that I used to catch in my mother's eyes when she was trying to help me do things.

I begin to play with the white, fluffy suds in the dishpan. I dip my hands into them, and I pick up a ball of tiny soap bubbles. I hold them up against the light, and in each of them I can see the brilliant colors of a miniature rainbow.

"Dear Lord," I whisper, "Our Father in heaven, I thank Thee, I thank Thee."

9 781088 284568